The Teachings of a Sufi Master

Seyed Mostafa Azmayesh

Mehraby Publications

The Teachings of a Sufi Master: Copyright © 2002 by Dr S. M. Azmayesh. All rights reserved to Seyed Mostafa Azmayesh. No part of this book may be reproduced or transmitted in any form or by any means, electronically or mechanical, including photocopying, recording, or by any information storage and retrieval system, without written permission from the author, except for brief quotations embedded in critics and reviews about this book.

The first edition was published in 2002 by the Simorg Sufi Society Inc, USA. The second edition (2016) is published by:

Mehraby Publishing House,
United Kingdom.
mehrabypublishinghouse@gmail.com

Copyright © Seyed Mostafa Azmayesh –2nd Ed, 2016.
ISBN 978-0-9558117-7-7

Special thanks to Mr. Mohammad Dananie, Mr. Steven Roushakes, and Dr. Ali Reza Analouei for their contributions and without whom publication of this book would not have been possible.

Publishers Note

Although many of the personal pronouns used in this book are masculine, they are not intended to exclude women. The Sufi teachings are inclusive of all human beings.

Figure 1- Rumi's Mausoleum, Konya, Turkey.

Contents

Introduction 9
    What is the Way of the Sufi? 10
    The Truth Lies in Your Heart 11
    Back to the Basis of Sufism 12
    The Mystical Teaching Method 13
    How Does One Recognise An Authentic School? 13
    What Is The Goal? 14
    Recipient Or Content? 16
    A Little Technique 19
    Less Egotistical, More Altruistic 21
    The Way Of The Parrot 22

Sheikh Kamel 25
    Uncle Hassan's Last Minutes 27
    The Mystery Of Death 29
    Death Is A Dream Without Return 32
    The Night Brings Counsel 32
    The Astral Voyages 34
    What Will Become of Uncle Hassan? 36
    The Aftermath Of The Voyage 38
    Time Does Not Have An Independent Reality 39
    School is Finished 42
    Have A Nice Trip, Uncle Hassan 45

The Nights of Ramadan 49
    1. The Two Doors 51
        A Few Words on Sufi Astrology 52
    2. The Bird in a Cage 55
    3. The Merchant and His parrot 61
        The Symbols 64
    4. The Two Worlds (Visible and Invisible) 67
        Dream or Reality 70

| The Beyond 70
| 5. The Interpretation of Dreams 75
| 6. The Old Wandering Musician 81
| Common Language or Collective Memory? 83
| 7. The Post-Physical World 87
| What about Reincarnation? 89
| The Dangers Of Idealising Reincarnation 94
| The One-Way Of The Two Doors 95
| 8. The Pre-Physical World 97
| The Broken Taboo 98
| 9. Escaping Death 101
| Suicide 101
| 10. Reality and Illusion 103
| The Shadow and the Bird 104
| The Deluded Cuckold 105
| The Influenced Professor 106
| The Elephant in the Dark 107
| 11. Meditation 111
| The Chinese And The Roman Artists 114
| 12. Explanation of the Principle of Negation 117
| There Is No Dervish (Sufi) In The World 118
| The Minstrel and the Turkish Emir 119
| Commentary 122
| 13. Soul Doctors 125
| The Bedouin And The Caliph Of Baghdad 127
| Mowlana's Message 129
| 14. An Allusion To The Principle Of Negation 131
| 15. The Grammarian And The Navigator 135
| The Grammarian and the Navigator 135
| 16. Man In The Image Of God 141
| The Deception Of Resemblance 142
| The Oil Merchant's Parrot 143

17. The Lion In The Desert And The Bowl Of Milk 147
    The Cow That Became A Lion 147
    The Lion's Meal 148
18. Wealth And Poverty 151
19. Thirty Birds 153
20. Ali Son Of Abu Taleb 155
21. Zekr 159
    The Influence Of Zekr 161
22. Fekr 165
    Majnoon And The Doctor 166
    The Unity Of The Lover And The Beloved 166
23. Moraghebeh (Meditation) 171
    Quarantine 171
    Mohassebeh – Self-Evaluation Of Our Actions 173
24. Hozeh 175
25. The Closing Of Schools Of Mysticism 179
26. The Truth About Jihad 183
    David And Goliath 185
27. Nafs 189
    The Distinction Between Jihads 190
28. The Story Of The Two Headed Creature 193

Introduction

Everyone is familiar with the whirling Sufis; more likely, everyone at some time has seen a film on Turkey and its folklore, where it is impossible to ignore the dances of the Sufis, dressed in long white robes and high felt headdresses, whirling to the monotonous rhythm of haunting music. Some know that the dervishes are originally mystics from the Middle East, whose roots are found in Islamic culture in a broad sense.

But very few know the real philosophy of the Sufis: the way of the Sufi.

Some think Sufism is an Islamic sect, which for them makes it suspicious and frightening. Others think it is just another Eastern religion, such as Zoroastrianism; Hinduism; or Buddhism.

However, Sufism is neither a sect nor a religion.

Sects are recognized by two main characteristics, easy to identify, which should stir suspicion: proselytism, that is, a constant search for new followers, and a tendency to extort money from its followers.

These characteristics go together: the more followers there are, the more money flows into the funds and into the pockets of leaders or so-called gurus.

Sufism by no means looks for new followers, though postulants are welcome. To follow the way requires no financial investment.

These two arguments should clear Sufism from any doubt or suspicion of sectarianism. Could it be a religion? A religion is characterised by dogmas, a set of beliefs officially established to which the follower must adhere to be a member of the "church" or community.

Sufism preaches no particular dogma, except the great truths that are the basis of all religious beliefs: the belief in the existence of divinity, of an invisible world, and of the immortality of the soul.

Unlike the mosque, the Sufi's gathering is open to all people; everybody can go in the circle of a Sufi Master as an observer without the need to change his religion. If you are Christian, Jewish, Buddhist, or even if you have no religion, your entrance to a Sufi gathering is not refused. Sufi circles are not exclusively for Muslims.

What is the Way of the Sufi?

Sufism is a set of personal practices – though rarely practiced collectively in small groups – designed to help the follower develop hidden and unexploited capacities, with the goal of developing knowledge of the self and the visible and invisible world, and guiding the seeker or "traveller" along the spiritual path, and ultimately acquiring truths of his existence and a certain vision of the world[1].

An enormous programme!

---

1 This definition is very close to the definition of yoga. The word yoga is most often misused nowadays, as it is generally used to define relaxation exercises. The Sanskrit definition of the word is "union." Real yoga has the purpose to produce the union of body, and soul, the union of the human being with the divinity and the universe. To reach this goal, yoga, like the Sufi way, many years of exercises, punctuated with successive spiritual stages that are always under the responsibility and guidance of a competent guide and master who knows all the stages, having experienced itself, are needed.

As a matter of fact, who would have the eccentric idea to start alone, without equipment, without training and without a map, to climb a dangerous and unknown glacier? Such a person would be foolish; he wouldn't have a one in a million chance to reach, intact, the top of the mountain to have a glimpse of the other side. Only with professional help of someone who knows all the traps, the places to rest and the shortcuts, can he be spared from failure or even from death. This is a warning to amateurs! Meditate on this analogy.

Introduction

The Truth Lies in Your Heart

The base postulate of Sufism, as with all mysticism, is that there is no need for blissful faith in a supposed truth, as advocated by dogmatic religions. All answers lie within the self, deep in the heart.

Sufism teaches the follower who sincerely seeks the truth to develop the capacities to discover for himself the answers to his existential questions. Thus, he draws his own truths, independent of any belief imposed or impressed upon him since childhood.

Have you ever asked yourself why you are Christian, for example?

Most likely, the majority would simply respond that they were born in the U.S.A. or in a European country into a Christian family. If you were born in the Middle East, you would probably be a Muslim; or a Buddhist, if you were born in Tibet! To what degree are you free to choose your religion? Unless you are converted, which is an exceptional case, you simply follow the religion of your parents, which mingles with traditions of your country and of your surroundings. When you think about it from a distance you realize the nonsense of religious wars.

Take the next step and go directly to the higher level and start with spiritual matters. What is essential is to have the will to progress on the way of essential evolution, to become better, more experienced and wiser. This will result in your time on Earth being positive. But we are going too quickly!

Back to the Basis of Sufism

A Sufi does not need to believe in the existence of unattainable mysteries. Every phenomenon has an explanation, every effect has a cause (and vice versa). Every human being is able to develop his soul until he attains the knowledge of what we call God (though we do not really know what this is). The only limits to an adequate learning method are found in our own capacities and in our personal work.

Let us linger for a while on these two fundamental points.

Each individual has a unique capacity. Although everyone has a chance to develop the soul, we must admit that, in this field, as in all of nature, equality does not exist. Some people have a small bicycle and must make an enormous effort to climb the mountain path; others are born with a big motorcycle that will carry them to the top without effort – if they are careful not to fall into a precipice. This is the reason why the Sufi way is individualised. Each person practices according to his own nature and capabilities. Teach the motorcyclist to pedal, and he will not get far. Teach the cyclist to start a motorcycle engine, and he will go nowhere! The type and rhythm of practices assigned to each person should be adapted to their actual state of mind and their aptitudes. This is why collective teaching is practically forbidden.

Personal exercise or work should be diligent and persistent. It is not a question of exhausting oneself for hours, but of practicing regularly each day for months, even years, before any perceptible result is felt. Here again, only the Sufi master, based on certain signs seen in meditation and in the dreams of the seeker, may evaluate the seeker's progress on the way to self-fulfilment and the development of his faculties.

The Mystical Teaching Method

One who sincerely seeks the way to substantial development, produces waves around himself, waves perceived by the teacher and the waves that show the seeker the techniques of esoteric self-interrogation. The teacher will appear at the right time in the life of the seeker.

As with any other profession, the postulant on the way to a substantial development must go through a systematic and well organised education. The authenticity of the mystical way is proven by its educational method. If a mystical school does not function accordingly, it is not authentic.

In each school, on a certain number of people are authorised to teach the technical practices of Sufism.

How Does One Recognise An Authentic School?

The link or connection to an ancient and well-established structure, based on a serious philosophical tradition, is the main proof of the authenticity of a Sufi school.

A true Sufi educational system never imposes any dogma or belief and never requires a renouncement of personal religious convictions. It is not based on religion but on spirituality and metaphysics.

The teacher never expects money, neither for his teaching, which are strictly individual, nor for his spiritual help. Those who sell paranormal abilities, such as clairvoyants, may very well have a real aptitude, but cannot be recognised as Sufis with authentic teaching methods. This indication is all-important and illustrates how to avoid the clutches of so-called gurus leading mercenary sects, and how to avoid falling under the spell of unscrupulous, self-proclaimed magi. They are numerous and they are dangerous!

Finally, the student will also recognize the authenticity of a school by the deep and meticulous teaching he is given, as well as by certain signs perceived in dreams.

The real spiritual adventure begins as the seeker becomes a traveller on the path to his own internal development and unity with his own spirit, the universe, and God.

What Is The Goal?

Looking at the definition of Sufism, we find a double purpose:

    (1) Personal development;

    (2) Knowledge of the self and of the visible and invisible world.

In fact, both purposes go hand-in-hand, because personal development leads to knowledge. This can be summarised under one definition that perfectly captures the Sufi goal: essential evolution.

This requires an explanation:

We human beings are not what we think we are. In reality, we are much more than what we think we are. Indeed, we each identify ourselves with our physical body, which was born some time ago from a father and a mother, somewhere on this earth. This physical body will die someday, as it is the ultimate destiny of all living creatures on this earth. When we declare, "I am John," we think of our physical person: its history, its health, its financial difficulties, its happy family, and everything that constitutes a daily life. This John – because we call him so – communicates with his environment through the five senses of his physical body: he sees with his eyes, hears with his ears, smells with his nose, tastes with his mouth, and uses his hands, or other parts of his body, to touch things. Thus, for him, the universe is exclusively made of what is accessible to his five senses

If a sound is inaudible for his ears, for example ultrasound, it might as well not exist, whereas his dog will perfectly hear and run to his master when John blows his ultrasound whistle, although this very whistle produces no perceptible sound for us human beings! Likewise, we know that some animals can perceive infrared and ultraviolet, which are colours unknown to the human eye because of our limited natural capacities. All this is to say that many things exist that remain inaccessible to the human beings because they are outside the reach of the five senses.

Because the five senses of our physical body allow us to perceive only the physical world, we tend to think that this is the only existing world; that we are this physical body because we feel the heartbeats in our chest.

Yet, it is not so!

There is an invisible world beyond the capacity of perception of our physical eyes, a world that is also inaudible – beyond our hearing capacities – and also impalpable, beyond all our five senses. But there are also many invisible worlds in such dimensions that make it impossible for us either to suspect their existence or even to define them. Words would be useless for the definition of what we cannot reach.

How can we describe colours to someone who is born blind? How can we describe the subtlety of music to someone who is born deaf and who has always lived in total silence? As long as we remain limited to our five senses, we have no idea of knowing a prairie in the invisible worlds.

Recipient Or Content?

Indeed the truth is that we are not only constituted of a mortal physical body with five senses that will perish with us at our death, but that each of us has also a soul or energetic body, invisible but immortal. This invisible body has five senses specific to its own world level; we can label this invisible world by the generic title *sixth sense*, in order to differentiate it from the five physical senses.

In our daily lives, our ordinary five senses dominate. The senses of the soul that inhabit our body are automatically switched off to such an extent that we even forget that we have a soul, that we are a soul that temporarily inhabits a body. Yet, as soon as the soul leaves the body, as it does when we dream, and definitively when we die, the five senses of the soul take over. This is the invisible world of the soul, where we shall all go someday, at the latest on the day of our death, our definitive departure from this earth.

Thus, during his lifetime on earth, the human being may be compared to a bird imprisoned in a small cage. The bird can stick its feet out between the bars in order to walk, but the cage is so narrow that its wings remain stuck to its body. The bird completely forgets that it has wings. It even forgets that it is a bird and believes that it is the cage, a moving cage with an internal mechanism.

This might sound amusing, but the soul is like a bird that could fly to infinite invisible worlds if it were not stuck in the material, physical body, which is a cage. We believe ourselves to be this limited physical body, whereas we are a soul-bird.

Introduction

The first goal of Sufism is to awaken the senses of the soul, named the sixth sense, and a range of other abilities related to the soul or energy of the body. These abilities seem to be supernatural or miraculous if you remain within the realm of the ordinary five senses, but they are the attributes of those who master their energetic bodies.

This is what we mean by "personal development." It is a question of consciously controlling and giving life to the abilities of the soul, while we inhabit our physical body. This requires long and sometimes dangerous training, but it can be done if one correctly follows an efficient teaching method.

In antiquity, one of the most important spiritual places in the Mediterranean was the temple at Delphi, seat of the celebrated Pythia oracle. There is an inscription on the pediment, written in classical Greek, with the following precept:

"Know yourself and you will know the universe and you will know God, and you will become God."

Sufi teaching has adopted this ancient maxim: by developing his soul's potential, the follower gains consciousness of his own aptitudes beyond his ordinary faculties. He acknowledges his real spiritual dimension. He acquires self-knowledge, and how to evaluate the possibilities of his energetic body. Thus, through personal and direct knowledge, he becomes certain of his immortality. Above all, he will recognise that he is a soul, or energetic body, temporarily contained inside a physical body for the duration of a lifetime. This certitude, born from his own direct experience, will give him not only great spiritual elation, but also a feeling of responsibility towards his fellow humans who never went through such experiences and who go on living in the complete ignorance of things beyond.

The follower will have experienced the crossing of the veil, what we call death because he lives outside of his physical body. He will come back, testifying that death is not an end, but only one stage; it is a change of vehicle to travel further, with vehicles better adapted to the circumstances.

For him there is no more anxiety or fear of death.

When the bird manages voluntarily to leave its cage, the animal realises that it is a bird and that it can fly. It stops identifying itself with the cage, and thus leaves the cage with ease.

Through personal experience and under the direction of a master, the follower may acquire direct experience of the universe beyond the reach of the five senses, using the faculty of his soul called the sixth sense, which he has developed for this purpose.

At this stage there is no longer any need to believe in dogmas. All veils fall, one by one, as the student learns more. According to the level of his maturity, he acquires answers to his questions. Throughout his apprenticeship, and through his personal experiences, he forms his own idea of the world, using his own visions, dreams or meditations. He attains this under the permanent guidance of his teacher who watches over him and leads him along this path full of pitfalls and hazards. To the seeker, this learning process knows no other limit than his capacities and personal work. Thus he can go as far as the end of the universe, as far as the ultimate truth, as far as the throne of God.

Introduction

A Little Technique

One can easily imagine that the awakening of the sixth sense is far from immediate. Noticing its first fleeting appearance, then mastering and using it, takes long years of spiritual practice articulated around some very old techniques that are to be found under various names in all mystic schools, from Indian yoga to the Tibetan lamas' initiation.

The physical senses must be put to sleep by means of the faculty of imagination, so that senses of the soul can emerge when then physical senses are pacified and numbed. The first technique, and probably the best known, is meditation. This is the act of depleting the spirit and successively neutralizing the ordinary senses until something triggers and tilts the spirit furtively into the other world, a world of dreams and visions, full of teachings and senses.

The second technique complements the first. It is concentration, which may be divided into two practices: visualisation (called *fikr* by the Sufis and *mandala* by the yogis); and mental repetition (called *zekr* by the Sufis and *mantra* by the yogis).

Visualisation uses mental projections, as detailed as possible, of a person, place, or other object. In general, the Sufi visualises his master, whose mental image he places in his heart, in himself, in order to identify with him.

The principle is that if the visualisations are correctly done, it comes to an invisible connection between the visualising and the object of visualisation; in this case, between the Sufi and his guide. This connection is fundamental, because as soon as the soul comes out of the body (in a state of meditation or in a dream), it joins the soul of the guide, in order to use its energy, wisdom and protection. This connection is one of the pillars of the Sufi's spiritual life. It leads to an immense spiritual love between master and student, as was, for example, the case between Mowlana Rumi and Shams of Tabriz[2].

Figure 2 - Shams Tabrizi's Tomb - Konya, Turkey.

Mental repetition, or *zekr*, consists of a short phrase repeated mentally a certain number of times, sometimes hundreds, according to the expected results. For the purpose of *zekr*, the Sufi generally holds a sort of rosary that he uses as a rhythmical support for his silent repetition. The principle here is that, in the long run, this repetition produces a vibration that can be very powerful, according to the chosen *zekr*. This vibration has very important effects on the

---

2 Jalāl ad-Dīn Muhammad Rūmī also known as Mawlānā and more popularly simply as Rumi was a 13th-century Persian poet, jurist, scholar, theologian, and a Sufi mystic. His poems have been widely translated into many languages. It was Rumi's meeting with his master Shams-e Tabrizi on 15 November 1244 that transformed Rumi from an accomplished teacher and jurist, into an ascetic.

Sufi and environment: heartbeats align with the rhythm of the *zekr*, and these vibrations act on certain endocrinal glands of the reptilian brain or paleo-cortex. This is the oldest and most primitive part of the brain, which controls, as its name suggests, such basic functions as hunger, temperature, sleep, as well as the primitive drives, such as sexuality and aggression.

Thus, a well-trained Sufi can completely control his physical body and his deepest drives.

He can put his senses to sleep in order to allow the emergence of his sixth sense. The combination of these methods makes it possible for him to sink, whenever he wishes, into a state of autohypnosis that immediately produces the exit of the soul from its physical prison.

Less Egotistical, More Altruistic

This conscientious control of the Sufi over his reptilian brain neutralises his animal and egotistical drives. This allows him to become a better person: less wild, more human; less egoistical and more altruistic; less materialistic and more spiritual.

This transformation is called the Essential Evolution. The Essential Evolution is, thus, an inner transformation, focused on the process of soul-making and away from all appearances.

Achievement of this evolution is the main goal of Sufism. Once all animal aspects are controlled, the Sufi is transformed: he is a new man who can leave his body whenever he wants and transport himself to those high levels. Through his connection to his master, he will be sent to seek counsel, to get help for his fellow men and for further progress towards self-knowledge and knowledge of the universe.

The Way Of The Parrot

To illustrate the way of the Sufi and clarify its principles, Mowlana Rumi, well known in the Western world, told this story:

There was a merchant who owned a beautiful parrot in a cage. As he was about to travel on business to India, the parrot said to him: "I would be very grateful if, once in India, you gave my greetings to the fellow birds that live there and if you told them that I live here in a cage." The merchant accepted this harmless request.

Once in India, he went to a big tree where a colony of multi-coloured parrots lived, birds very similar to his own. As promised, he delivered the greeting. As soon as he had finished speaking, one of the parrots fell to the ground and remained there, inert. Our merchant was very impressed by this. As he came back home, very embarrassed and very sorry that he might have caused the death of a beautiful Indian parrot, he told his own bird what had happened. At that moment his parrot fell off its perch, apparently subject to a sudden cataleptic stroke.

Our merchant took the bird out of the cage and left it on the ledge of the window, meaning to bury it later in the garden.

He was aghast when he saw the beautiful bird fly away to the nearest tree and express its gratitude with these words:

"You told me about your experience with my fellow birds in India, and you have passed on their message, telling me how to get out of my prison. Without knowing it, you have extended to me the secret of my liberation. Thank you, my friend!"

Introduction

This little story, like many Sufi stories, is rich in symbols and teachings. To be taught how to free itself, the soul (the parrot), which is prisoner of the body (the cage), tries to contact other spirits (the Indian parrots) that are free from all earthly bounds and living in the other world (India). At this stage, the soul, which has no other way to communicate directly with the beyond, must use its capacity of deduction as a communication tool (the merchant). The method indicates the necessity to annihilate egotism and egocentrism.

Because of this short story the way of the Sufi is called "the way of the parrot."

Figure 3 – A Sufi Sama gathering[3]

---

[3] Public domain picture (1892)

https://archive.org/details/popularsciencemo41newy

Sheikh Kamel

Uncle Hassan's Last Minutes

Uncle Hassan is about to die. He has spent the last two months in the hospital, dragging himself from bed to armchair, from armchair to bed. Now he is bedridden. It all started with an infection of the urinary tract, which couldn't be treated. The tract became infected, and the infection went to the lungs. Uncle Hassan has problems breathing and he suffers from high fever. He hardly eats and survives only with intravenous drops in each arm. Aunt Pooneh is anxiously waiting. The doctor came by yesterday and shook his head, which spoke volumes of his prognosis. Aunt Pooneh had bombarded him with questions. He said it wouldn't be long now, just a question of days; the immune system is exhausted.

His two children have come as fast as they could. Sara comes from the seaside where she lives. She usually comes once or twice a year, for the New Year and for summer vacations. She has crossed the desert and the mountains, just to come to his bedside. Tired from the trip and heavy emotions, she has dark circles under her eyes. The death of a loved one is a serious and solemn moment in life, it takes you by the heart; it brings up the real questions: What comes next? Is this really the end? Will we ever meet him again? Her father breathes faster; she feels dizzy. Uncle Hassan is half conscious. He notices the presence of his beloved family by his side, but the drugs they have given him has blurred his mind, which is already numbed by fever, anaemia, and exhaustion. Aunt Pooneh is deep in prayer. Her eyes closed, she concentrates and prays in a mechanical way as if trying to divert her mind from this sad reality to give her courage.

Aunt Pooneh believes in God. She believes in the way of our grandmothers, with an unshakable faith handed down through centuries of religious education, as most people in her birth city of Shiraz. In this ancient city, modernity and ancestral traditions live side-by-side in complete harmony. The mausoleum of a great religious person, Shah Cheragh, is in the centre of the city. There are other graves in the suburbs, where great mystics, such as S'adi[4], Hafez[5], and Khadjoo[6], are buried. The people of Shiraz, although very modern, are mostly believers. They believe in life after death, when body and soul part. Our Aunt Pooneh has no doubt Hassan will rise at the end of time, to be together in paradise with the blessed, the prophets and all the saints "who continually sing the hymn in praise of His glory." This is what she has learned in her childhood.

But the end of time is so far! Deep in her heart, she is worried: she is afraid of death, of separation, of solitude. Hassan is disturbed and tries to catch his breath. His exhausted heart gives way. The heart rate monitor's wave becomes flat; a shrill alarm sounds. The surveillance nurse rushes in, but all she can do is notice that there is nothing more to do. Aunt Pooneh weeps at the foot of the bed. She holds her daughter Sara in her arms. This is the end of fifty years of married life, in this depressing and anonymous hospital room. There are now a number of problems to solve: what to wear, planning of the funeral, calling friends and family, the frightening act of going to the cemetery and coming back

---

4 Abū-Muhammad Muslih al-Dīn bin Abdallāh Shīrāzī better known by his pen-name Saadi was one of the major Persian Sufi poets and literary men of the thirteenth century.

5 Khwāja Shams-ud-Dīn Muḥammad Ḥāfeẓ-e Shīrāzī known by his pen name Hafez, was a famous Sufi poet of the fourteenth century and his collected works are regarded as a pinnacle of Persian literature.

6 Khadjoo was a Sufi master, poet and the teacher of Hafez.

to an empty house where each detail will be a reminder of their happy years together. Aunt Pooneh is drained, she suddenly feels very weak.

The Mystery Of Death

At the moment when Hassan takes his final breath, emotion has reached its peak and the members of the family have tears in their eyes. Sheikh Kamel is a very old Sufi, a man of experience with many disciples. Hassan was one of them. When Hassan passes, the Sheikh observes how a blue wreath comes out of the deceased's abdomen, at the level of the solar plexus, forming a cloud like the smoke of a cigarette. He then sees how this elongated cloud takes a human form, like a clone of the lifeless body, and floats slowly under the ceiling, above Hassan.

Sheikh Kamel thinks that if Aunt Pooneh knew the truth, she wouldn't be so desperate. If she could observe frequencies invisible to the human eye, she would have seen how Hassan's smoky double had left the dead body. She would know for sure that death is not an end but a change of state, which is not the opposite of life, but the opposite of birth. She would learn that physical death is a birth in the other world. Sheikh Kamel decides to comfort the poor old woman. He asks her to sit next to him. He explains that there is no need to wait for an eventual end of time: crossing the veil is immediate and totally painless. This is generally experienced as liberation after a long agony, as release from all the bodily hindrances on a tired and deficient physical body. When death comes, the soul (or energetic body) leaves the physical body which has become useless, just in the same way as the way a driver would leave an old vehicle with a burned motor on the side of the road, before going on his own way.

Sheikh Kamel is a much respected, and an exceptional figure. He is old in years, but young at heart. Although very attached to traditions, he understands the needs of modern people very well. He knows the Qur'an by heart. Besides the time he spends in meditation and other esoteric practices, he reads scientific books and magazines. He loves music: classical music of the Western world and his own, traditional national music. He also loves Sufi music, the Indian sitar and the flute used by the South American Indians. He himself can play some traditional Persian instruments, though he never plays in public. He reads texts in Arabic, English, French, and of course Persian, his native tongue. He has written many books about Sufism and mysticism, for every type of public, but primarily addressed to young people and academics. Among his followers are French, Dutch, British, American, African – Muslim and people practicing other religions. He is friendly and easy to approach. There is an atmosphere of love, trust, friendship and fraternity around him. He often repeats that because God has created us from one and the same pair, we are all sisters and brothers. We must therefore help and understand one another. He constantly advises his disciples to always be helpful and never try to dominate others. He often reminds his audience that the more devout and helpful they are, the dearer they are to the saints and to God's friends. The people who associate with him think that he has a positive influence on the city, and even on the world.

When he speaks, there is total silence; people listen very carefully. He knows many Persian poems; he has also seriously studied the deeper aspects of the occult in Persian poetry. He knows the philosophical and mystical texts written by great Eastern personalities. He has also authored comparative studies of various monotheistic religions. He has produced a very argumentative essay about the continuity of esoteric and Gnostic currents in Iran, from the Mazdean to the Shiite era.

He carefully follows the evolution of computer sciences and the new media, as well as the natural sciences. The spectacle of science coming ever closer to faith makes him very happy. Very wise and with a huge a reserve of knowledge, he is very tolerant with those who ignore spirituality. Yet he never wastes an occasion to show people to the right way to substantial perfection. In this respect, he now takes the opportunity to clarify the mystery of death for Hassan's family. He invites them to his house and gives them more explanations. He says:

"We generally believe ourselves to be made of a physical body, because this is the only one we can perceive with our five senses when we are awake. Each of us has many bodies, invisible ones, which are piled on top of the physical body, like a Russian doll, but each on a different wavelength." He quotes Mowlana Jalal'din Balkhi Khorasani (the famous Persian Sufi known in the Western world as Mowlana Rumi)[7]

> *You have, in addition to the visible body, other bodies.*
>
> *Why do you fear the leaving of your soul?*

As Aunt Pooneh questions the possibility of two bodies in a single space, Sheikh Kamel simply says that the subtle essence of the energetic body merges with elements constituting the physical body like water in a sponge! The energetic body vibrates on a higher wavelength than the physical body, so that the normal human eye can't see it. He continues, "Have you ever seen a cat react as if facing some invisible opponent, curving its back, stretching out its claws, its hair bristling up? This simply happens because the cat is facing a frightening entity or simply one that it doesn't like. Some animals can see a much wider range of frequencies than we. In reality, cats have much sharper perceptions than we, and if they could talk, they would have strange things to tell us!"

---

[7] Masnavi Mirkhani, vol.3, Tehran, 1953, p.273.

Death Is A Dream Without Return

Sheikh Kamel explains:

"During our life, our energetic body, or what the occultists call the "astral body," overlaps the physical body, but we are not aware of its existence. When we fall asleep, the astral body moves out of the physical body, to which it remains tied through a kind of long elastic band of vibratory nature called "the silver cord," because this is what the seers observe. This silver cord is attached to the physical body at the level of the solar plexus, under the stomach, at a place where some emotions and strong sensations are felt, such as a twisting and twirling movement, as when we ride a carousel."

The Night Brings Counsel

Sheikh Kamel explains that Sufi teaching is based on the method of self-exploration, as described in sacred texts such as the Old and the New Testament, as well as in the Qur'an. According to the Quranic verses, the physical body recovers strength in sleep. At the same time, simultaneously, the astral body lives its own life in an invisible world, which is in fact its natural habitat (see the later tale of The Old Acrobat). Most of the time, the astral body remains close to the physical body and produces its own fantasies born from the sleeper's daily worries. Sometimes we wake up remembering to have dreamed some meaningless dreams, which are nothing but the product of our own mind.

Sometimes the astral body leaves, still connected to the physical body by the silver cord, which shines in the dark of night. It visits countries far away, other planets, and even invisible worlds. This can happen in the present, past, or future. Time is not a hindrance in the invisible worlds.

Sheik Kamel then recites poems of the third volume of the Masnavi Mowlana Jalal'din Balkhi Khorasani[8]:

He slept and the bird of his soul escaped its prison

Leaving behind the musician and his instrument, it set itself free

Thus it became free from the body and free from the tortures of the world

Roaming in the universe of tranquillity, in the middle of a spiritual landscape

His soul in that world said:

If they would leave me as I please in these surroundings

I would look all around, without needing eyes

I would pick roses and flowers, without using hands

I would travel all over, without needing feet or wings

I would eat sweets, without needing a mouth or teeth

I would sit in Zekr and Fekr sessions with the inhabitants of

Yonder, without being subject to headaches and worries

Because this earth and these skies, in spite of their immensity, are so narrow.

That they have torn my heart in sorrow

Yet, the world they have shown to me

has opened up my eyes to its greatness

If that world and the way to it were accessible

Not one second would anyone remain down here

---

8 Pub. Mirkhani /Tehran 1953/ page 51

The Astral Voyages

Sheikh Kamel continues:

"You must know that the astral body has the ability to fly and glide, carried by the network of electromagnetic currents that exist in the universe. It moves like a seagull that uses the wind currents. Everyone remembers having sometime dreamed he was flying over real or imaginary landscapes. These dreams are the "astral voyages."

Our astral body can bring back especially enriching experiences, answers to important problems or premonitory dreams that will help the dreamer to escape danger or make choices.

This is the meaning of "the night brings counsel," as the old popular wisdom says. When the dreamer wakes, the astral body quickly returns to the physical body, where it falls with breath-taking speed. Did you ever wake up with a start, with the feeling of having fallen from a very high altitude, from a cliff or into a shaft? This is due to the hasty return of your astral body to its vehicle."

Once more Sheikh Kamel recites a verse of the Qur'an to illustrate that at the time of death, the astral body is expelled from the physical body, just as it is in sleep. The only difference is that the silver cord begins to turn black at the point of junction to the dead physical body. Then it breaks definitively and begins to dissolve. Consciousness remains numbed for a while, sometimes as long as three days. Then the "living dead" awakes in his new state and begins to experiment the functionalities of his astral body. He often does not know that he is dead. It may sound strange, but he ignores everything about death and the laws of the invisible world. As his passage has been painless and unconscious, the deceased thinks he is still on our poor old Earth and tries to return to normal life with his family, especially if he has died young and violently. On the seventh day, he comes back home to visit his family, then he returns to his non-material world.

Sheikh Kamel is not only a specialist of Quranic studies; he is also very familiar with the mystical currents of the large religions. He says that in the Christian scriptures, Saint Paul writes about the energetic body, which he qualifies as heavenly and incorruptible[9]. This is sometimes expressed in confusing words, because of the translation. The idea of the vibratory quality of wavelength is described as "brilliance," which is also true. The energetic body is surrounded with a luminous halo created by its own electromagnetic field (also called the "aura"). It refers to the luminous halo around the head of saints. The Sheikh quotes Saint Paul for Aunt Pooneh and the other members of Uncle Hassan's family:

But, we will ask, how do the dead revive themselves?

With which body? Mad question!

The seed that you sow only gives life if it begins by dying.

That which you sow is different from the plant to come…

…Not all flesh is alike…

…Similarly there are celestial bodies and terrestrial bodies;

but the brilliance of some is different from others.

The same is true for the resurrection of the dead.

Sown corruptible, the body is reborn incorruptible…

…Sown as a simple human body, it takes life again transformed by the Spirit,

---

9 I Corinthians, 15:35-37.

What I want to say, brothers, is that flesh and blood

cannot inherit the kingdom of God and that which is mortal be incorruptible.

What Will Become of Uncle Hassan?

Sheikh Kamel then quotes a passage of the Masnavi[10]:

Through my experience I have understood

That death is life in the prison of the body;

Later, it will be the ultimate liberation and immortality.

A few days later, the village mosque is completely full. The whole family is here for the ceremony and all the villagers too. The elderly have known Hassan since their youth, as they all went to school together. Some people have come out of politeness, in sympathy to Aunt Pooneh and to pay last respects to the deceased. Others have come out of curiosity; funerals are occasions to see other people and later gossip with neighbours and shopkeepers.

In the first rows sit the cousins who came from Tabriz, though they had not been heard from for the last ten years. With their dark clothes and polished shoes, they really look proper! Everybody stands up and Sheikh Kamel goes to a small dais. He invites them to listen. He begins, "We have come here together to pay our last respects to Hassan; but Hassan is also present. He is here and sees everything from above; he floats up there, in a corner of the ceiling next to a column. He is perplexed; he does not realise what is going on. When you sing a religious song, he thinks, 'Funerals are fun, because you see so many people again.' He is here and wonders, 'But who is being

---

10 Mowlana / Masnavi / vol. 6 / p.640

buried today?' He is amazed, to be floating high up near the column. He thinks, 'This is a crazy situation, I must be dreaming.'"

Sheikh Kamel stops a moment to catch his breath. Then he says, "Hassan is here; he sees his wife sitting in the first row, crying and almost collapsing. But he really does not understand what is going on. He believes Pooneh is crying for the death of some very close person. He is very upset to see her in such a state, but he does not know how to comfort her."

A few hours later, they come together in the cemetery that surrounds the little mosque. They gather around an open grave.

Hassan now begins to recall memories of his life. He remembers the sad hospital room, the smiling nurse behind his oxygen mask, Pooneh, her tense face, sitting at the foot of his bed. He wonders, "Am I dead? Can this be? No, I am alive, I must be dreaming."

After the funeral, Hassan tries to talk to Pooneh. Seeing indifference on her face, he decides to take her hand. He is bewildered when his hand crosses hers, as if she did not exist, feeling only a light prickling, a sensation similar to passing through fog on an early winter morning. Now Hassan realizes that he is beyond the veil. "What will become of me? I am not going to drag myself like a lonely soul, without anyone to talk to. Oh God! Do something!" Then he feels a presence by his side. His master has come to guide him yonder to his future residence.

The next day, Aunt Pooneh asks about her husband, and the Sheikh tells her not to worry.

"He is under my protection. He has been a good Sufi. The pact between us will always be valid, in both the visible and invisible worlds. He has been well received in the other world. He was accompanied by a very powerful person who radiated a golden light. He has been taken to wide landscapes where his parents, Sufis and saints have been waiting for him. He felt irresistibly attracted to a luminous point in the sky, where he has thrown himself, as though drawn by a powerful current, in a dazzling tunnel of light."

Sheikh Kamel stops talking. He tries, with a movement of his head, to point out that he was this guiding person. In fact, as an advanced spiritual master, he is on both levels. He can show himself on one level and act at the same time in the other world.

The Aftermath Of The Voyage

In one of the Sufi gatherings, on a Thursday evening, Sheikh Kamel provides more details about Hassan's fate:

"Hassan must be an example for us. He was good, honest, and without problems. He always acted according to his conscience. He noticed his new state very fast and his transition to a better residence was easy. It is not always the case for the new dead, who are in fact the new born, if you look at it another way!

Each one goes to the beyond with no other luggage than the experiences gathered in life on earth. Everything we have done, good or bad, leaves traces on our energetic body. The balance of our actions and our thoughts gives our astral body a very personal level of vibrations. The more the subject has been a materialist, an egoist, violent and criminal, the weaker his vibrations. Religious people will speak of a soul charged with the weight of its sins. On the other hand, the more the subject has been spiritual and altruistic, kind and peaceful, the higher the vibrations of his astral body. In this case, the soul will be light and will want to quit this earth earlier for a better residence.

This is the real meaning of the scaling of souls, which determines the deceased's destination after death. This happens automatically: each individual goes where his vibrations pull him."

Sheikh Kamel quotes a hadith, which, according to the prophet of Islam, was expressed by his spiritual brother and predecessor, Jesus:

'My Father's kingdom has many mansions.'

Time Does Not Have An Independent Reality

Sheikh Kamel is a perfect Sufi but also a modern man, living in his time. Once in a while, in his speeches, he mentions new scientific discoveries to illustrate his declarations on mysticism. To explain the reality of the visible and invisible worlds, he uses the example of television:

"There are many channels, each broadcasting different and independent programmes. From the highly cultural to the most stupid, from the most violent to the most educational, they all exist side-by-side on your TV. When you look at your favourite programme on the first channel, you do not see what the other channels are showing. To change channels, you must use a remote control, which is the object replacing the good old round buttons we had twenty years ago. But this does not stop the second channel from broadcasting prayers and the third from showing a documentary on sturgeon fishing in the Caspian Sea. All this happens simultaneously to your programme of choice. Let us imagine that you have lost the remote control, or worse, that you never had one. Then you only have one channel and you do not know about the 130 other channels that could be received!

This demonstrates the absurdity of the notion of 'time.'

In a defined time, let us say one hour, you are exposed to a compilation of the broadcasting time of all the 130 channels that simultaneously broadcast various programmes. If you have six channels and only one hour, five hours of other programmes remain invisible. If you have, through cable or satellite, 130 channels, when you look at one channel during one hour, 129 programmes remain hidden. This means that during one hour, a multitude of things happen in parallel. We see through this explanation the immensity of our inadequacy to understand sensible events. Thus, what can we say about facts beyond the comprehension of our five senses?

In our example, each channel corresponds to a frequency used by the TV station. The station sends waves that circulate in the atmosphere, all around us; we do not notice them. The TV is only a device that the antenna concentrates into sounds and images, showing for example a reporter live at the other end of the world, or recorded images taken by a camera.

We are used to it now; it all seems so matter of fact. But in reality, isn't this magic?

The world in which we live is like a huge TV. But the faculties of our physical body limit us to only one channel. You will understand that this does not mean that there are no other channels. We simply do not have the remote control that would allow us to change the channel.

Our physical body vibrates on a given and rather low frequency, which is the frequency of our old physical world. The physical body cannot free itself from this wavelength. On the other hand, the energetic body, which is our vehicle when we dream, and especially when we die, has the capacity to travel on a range of frequencies. If we use the example of the TV again, which I find very significant, the energetic body has the capacity to change channels.

To use a remote control, you must first read the instructions manual and then train a little. The recently deceased generally do not have the slightest idea about what to expect. They simply wander to where their natural wavelength takes them."

After this comparison, Sheikh Kamel resumes with another illustration:

"Imagine an elevator, very light and precise, and that in this elevator, the lighter the passenger the higher it goes. A very heavy person will produce, under the force of gravity, a downward movement towards the basement. This should give you a rough image of what happens after death: if the soul in the astral body is light, that is, if the person has a clear and peaceful conscience and if he has done good on earth, his level of vibrations will rise. Once set free from the dead body he is going to go up, and the "magical" elevator will go to a higher plane, where only people with the same vibrations the same quality of soul, have access. An old proverb says: 'those who resemble, assemble.' Your alcoholic neighbour who was envious and slanderous, has no way to come here and disturb you. His vibrations are too low; his sins put weight on his soul. When such a person dies, in the best case, the lift doesn't move.

The poor man wanders around like a lonely soul in a world where he finds no access to anything. He will go to bars where no one will see him and no one will serve him a drink. He will haunt his house and see his children waste his money. This goes on until he perhaps understands that he had wasted his time on Earth and could have done better than just bothering the neighbours. If he does finally understand,-then maybe some help will come from above, and he will be raised one or two levels.

In the worst case, if he has truly produced devastation by egotism, violence and meanness, his level of vibrations will be so low that the lift will automatically go down to a level called hell by religious people. This place is not a place of eternal damnation, but simply a place where the vibrations are very low and unpleasant. Only bad people come here – those who go on with their vice, who hurt each other permanently, because it is their nature to act this way. Sometimes they get a chance to move out, to make up for their past life on Earth and to try to elevate their soul a bit.

In truth, each one will get what he deserves. Those who discreetly do good will go up. Those who deceive and do bad, giving the impression to be winners on Earth, are automatically dispatched to their legitimate place, as soon as they have crossed the veil.

It is only a question of time..."

School is Finished

Sheikh Kamel does not use complicated words. He prefers to tell anecdotes, tales and legends. He also uses concrete examples. He knows a lot of poems by Hafez, Mowlana, Sa'di and other masters and mystical poets by heart. It is because of this richness and simplicity that people love the old man and make sure not to miss his speeches. When Sheikh Kamel speaks, followers record his words on cassettes, to listen to them later, over and over again.

His speeches take place during Sufi sessions three times a week, on Tuesday evening, Friday at dawn, and Sunday evening. They begin with joint prayers, and after each prayer the Sheikh leads liturgies. These are individual prayers that the Sufis learn from their master. They vary in number and in nature for each person (we will return to this matter later).

At the end of each session, the Sheikh bows his forehead to the floor, to request the benediction of his Lord. The followers do the same. Then the Sufis stand in a circle and look at their master. One of them reads a Sufi text, a subject for reflection. Then a Sufi recites mystical poems. There is no music or group repetition of the names of God. Each does his silent work, as Sheikh Kamel has taught him. He repeats in his head one of the names of God, while controlling his breath and his imagination, putting all his attention on his heartbeats. At the end of the session, this can take almost two hours, the Sufis one by one shake the hand of Sheikh Kamel and kiss him as a sign of allegiance and brotherhood. This is how each Sufi gathering comes to an end.

During these sessions Sheikh Kamel speaks of spirituality and the travel of the soul in various worlds:

"Have you ever asked yourself what we are doing on this earth? The question makes you dizzy: Who am I? Where do I come from? Where am I going? In what state do I wander?

In reality, our old Earth is a school.

One lifetime is like a school year where each one has a programme, following general learning lines, and learning things we could not otherwise learn, because we are prisoners of ignorance in a physical body with limited possibilities.

When the school year is over, we have a grand vacation!

There you are, the nature of life on earth, which is like a school year, and of death (or rather, life after death), which is like the relationship of school time to vacation.

The soul is allowed a little rest before it goes to higher grade, provided it has learned the lessons of his school plan. We usually do not find out about this program during our lifetime on Earth. Just as in school, the teacher is the only one who knows the programme and who can evaluate whether we are making progress at the right speed. This programme consists of the many ordeals to which every human life is successively confronted. These are the things that build our soul. They are enriching experiences that make us, in general, wiser, though there are always exceptions. We are wiser in old age than we are at twenty, when we are full of illusions, first entering the cruel world of adults.

It is well known that comfort and facility soften. Remember Hannibal's army and the delights of Capua! Difficulties build up and elevate a soul, just as metal hardens through steeping. To become solid and good for the fighting, the metal sword will be heated red-hot then immediately dipped into cold water. It is the ordeal of temperature difference that makes the sword indestructible.

Ordeals, however, must be proportional to the capacities and the real needs of each soul. In principle this must be the case, though it is not always apparent."

Have A Nice Trip, Uncle Hassan

After a short break, the wise man continues:

"Death, as such, is absolutely not difficult for the one concerned; it is no more than quietly falling asleep and having a nice dream, without return. What is difficult is not death, but the suffering that often occurs when the body is seriously ill and at the end of its forces.

Another fear is the idea of leaving behind loved ones. But time goes faster there, in the beyond, than here on Earth: the waiting time does not seem long. If he makes progress on the other side, the recently deceased will be able to help, unseen, loved ones left behind on Earth. He will help by preventing dangers, interceding through higher powers; he will prepare and participate in the important events in the life of those left behind and for whom he is actively waiting.

In fact the departed will not spend eternity seated on a cloud in a long white robe with golden wings and playing the harp, 'continually singing the hymn to His glory along with a choir of angels,' according to popular beliefs. There is much to do there! You must progress toward more knowledge and spirituality, but above all you must help others to solve their problems and make progress, as well.

A huge programme! An eternity is needed to do all this!

The most difficult situation is for the survivors who share the agony of the dying person and who must later part from the loved one: the wife who remains alone in life; the small children who become orphans. There are so many painful experiences, which sometimes seem very difficult to overcome and make us doubt the limits of our own resistance.

Most survivors do not know the things discussed here.

They completely ignore everything of the other world.

Their distress is all encompassing.

They should know that the physical body is just a vehicle that makes it possible for us to live in the physical world, and that the soul dressed in the energetic body is like a car the driver abandons on the roadside when the engine is finally broken and beyond repair.

Think about this when you wake up in the morning and remember having flown in the skies or having brutally fallen down, with a strange sensation in your stomach.

Also remember how it feels after having been in an uncomfortable position. You have the impression to have lost control of a limb; it feels now rigid and swollen. The persistent prickling sensation that generally follows is the sign of normalisation. The reason is that the corresponding energetic limb spontaneously detaches from the physical limb. The prickly sensation shows that the energetic body is coming back to its normal place, as in waking, superposed to the physical limb.

Think about all this when you are confronted with death. Have the certitude that:

WE ARE ALL IMMORTALS"[11]

---

[11] What you have read here is explained in detail by the great Sufi Sheikh Sadr-din-Shirazi, known as Mollah Sadra in his main work, Asfar. This Arabic word means "books" (plural of sefr) and also "travels" (plural of safar). Afsar is a text composed in four chapters, each chapter corresponding to the travel of the soul in one of the worlds: before physical birth, during life in the physical body, in the intermediate

Sheikh Kamel pauses, and then adds, "Tomorrow is the first day of the month of Ramadan. We will use this time to explore the subject of soul travel in various worlds."

world after death, and in the supernatural world after having been judged for its deeds. Afsar is a very technical and very rich book, based on two forms of logic: "borhan-e-arshi," which covers his own visions, and "borhan-e-ahgli," the author's rational deductions.

The same notion of the travel of the soul has been developed in Dante's The Divine Comedy, which is practically the exact translation of an Islamic manuscript called Meradj Nameh, which describes the mystical travel of the Prophet of Islam in supersensible worlds.

Many other Sufi authors have developed the Sufi point of view. Examples include Aboi Madjid Madjdoud ibn Adam Sanai in his book Sir ol Ebad Menal Mabda Elal Morud, Sheikh Nadjedin Razi in his book Mersad ol Ebad menal mabadtelal motad. Sufism does not acknowledge reincarnation. Among great Sufi masters who have explicitly addressed the question of reincarnation, while seriously criticising and condemning the notion of it, we can name Sheikh Alao Dowleh Semnani. Nowadays, the question of life after death is no more a mystery. Have you seen the film Ghost? It shows what can happen after death, and shows rather precisely the deceased in his astral body, trying to communicate with his family and succeeding only through a medium. Seeing this film is recommended, after having read the story of the poor Hassan.

Also Dr. Raymond Moody's book Life After Life is recommended. Dr. Moody has focused his study on the accounts of those who have come close to the great voyage only to come back in extremis, a situation also called "NDE" (Near Death Experience).

The Nights of Ramadan

1 - The Two Doors

The first day of the month of Ramadan is coming to an end. This day will be followed by twenty-nine other days where the Sufis will fast, provided their health permits. From dawn to sunset they will not eat or drink; this is a very good practice, and relatively efficient, to develop resistance against instinctive human impulses.

In spite of his advanced age, Sheikh Kamel fasts this year, like every other year. Besides, he fasts regularly, twice a week, on Thursdays and Fridays.

The Sufi sessions take place every day during this month. Every morning they gather at dawn to pray under the master's guidance. They will come together again later, for the other four prayers of the day: midday, afternoon, sunset and at nightfall. Occasionally, one of the Sufis – or even one who does not belong to the circle – will invite them all to a banquet.

During the weekly gatherings, Sheikh Kamel continues to preach and designates the evenings to develop his explanation of the way the soul moves within the material world and in the two universes before and after it. On this first night of Ramadan he begins thus:

"The existential question that occupies each of us may be summarised as: 'Who am I? Where do I come from and where am I going?'

We cannot pretend to have answers to these questions, but we can draw knowledge from Sufi masters. The masters teach us that there is immediately beyond the physical world (called *Ja* in Persian), two other worlds that affect us directly: the pre-physical world (*Ja Bolga*) and the post-physical world (*Ja Bolsa*).

Each of these worlds is connected to our world through a tunnel. The pre-physical world is situated east of nature, the place where souls start in direction of elementary bodies. The post-physical world is situated west of nature, towards where the soul goes after it has parted from the physical body. The human being has therefore three lives: life before the body, life inside the body, and life after the body. The coming together between body and soul occurs as an accident, like when a bird is caught in a trap."

A Few Words on Sufi Astrology

The Sheikh continues:

"When Providence wishes that a soul enter a body, material elements and cosmic bodies become active.

According to Sufi masters, when one spermatozoid fertilises an ovum, this first stage of conception is subject to the influence of the moon. This influence remains predominant during the first month of pregnancy.

During the second month, Mercury watches over the maturing foetus. Then comes Venus, before the Sun takes over for one month at the end of the third month. During the third week of the fourth month, under the supervision and influence of the Sun, the soul comes inhabits the foetus.

On this point, the mystic masters have various interpretations. Some believe that the soul had existed indefinitely before the foetus is even conceived. Others think that the soul is created at the same time as the foetus. Mullah Sadra Shirazi confirms that the soul has two existences: one that it is timeless, but its attachment to the body coincides with the constitution of the foetus. On the other hand, Nassir Eddin Tussi maintains the opposite. He believes that the soul is a product of the body that its creation begins at the time of conception, but after birth it is eternal.

The common point to all these theories is the residence of the soul in the physical body: the masters are all convinced that the soul resides in a point placed deep in the heart. The heart is situated at the fourth level of the energetic anatomy, and the fourth month of pregnancy belongs to the Sun; there is a special relationship between the heart and the Sun. During the fifth month, the growing foetus is under the influence of Mars, then Saturn during the next month. At the seventh month, the moon takes over again. If the child were to be born during the seventh month, it would most likely live because the moon's nature is humid and cold, qualities that are in direct relation to the nature of life.

At the eighth month, the foetus again comes under the influence of Saturn, whose characteristics, cold and dry, correspond to the nature of death. In case of a premature birth in the eighth month, the child will only survive if it is kept under permanent medical care until the ninth month. At the beginning of the ninth month, the foetus comes under the supervision of Jupiter, whose nature is warm and humid, like the essence of life. This is the reason why a child born in the ninth month will remain, in principle, alive and in good health. Because of all these influences, the seven celestial bodies: the sun, the moon and the five satellite planets, are called the cosmological fathers. The four structural elements of the physical body are called the 'quadrimothers.'

The conception of the physical body, the emergence into life, and the emanation of the soul occur with the complicity of the four mothers and the seven fathers!"

2 - The Bird in a Cage

Tonight Sheikh Kamel resumes his teaching. He begins with quotations from Avicenna, Sohrevardi, and other great masters of the mystic:

"The human soul is compared to a magnificent talking bird, a parrot, pushed by providence into the trap of the material world.

Why this comparison?

Because the soul has the capacity to fly like a bird. It can fly in the skies of this world, as well as in the 'heavens', the invisible world, where the departed souls reside, or simply during sleep in a dream phase.

Unlike the physical body, the soul is not governed by the law of gravity. When a soul is out of its body, it has a tendency to float and glide on magnetic currents, like seagulls. Seagulls use the ascending currents to rise without effort over the water and search for fish. In a similar process, the gliding soul, no longer hindered by gravity or the five senses of the physical body, attains an infinitely vast view of the surrounding world. Like a bird living in captivity in a cage, the soul is prisoner of the body. At birth, the soul, originating from the pre-physical world, symbolized by the Indies, in Sufi imagery falls into the body, as when the bird is trapped in a cage that will not let it consciously free before its death.

When the cage is worn down, the bird will be able to escape definitively, rich with the experiences it has attained as a bird in a cage. Thus, death and the end of the physical body give the soul the freedom to travel in the vast world of the souls.

During physical life, the individual identifies with his own body, considering himself physically alive. This is the same as the parrot so used to being imprisoned that identifies with the cage, talking to it as if it was himself.

When death arrives, the soul leaves the body, never to return. But, because the soul is accustomed to inhabiting a body, it often continues to think of itself as a physical being. Because the soul takes the exact form of the body it has occupied during the physical life, its true nature is difficult to apprehend. If we meet a close acquaintance in a dream, he generally looks as he did during his normal life. In such a meeting, the two souls, out of their physical bodies, have exactly the same forms, the same characteristics, and the same physical dimensions as their physical persons, sleeping in their bed. Because the transition from wakefulness to dreaming is unconscious, the mind is incapable of distinguishing between these two states. Thus, in sleep we are not aware that we are dreaming.

It is the same after death: one is generally not conscious of being dead, continuing to think and act as if still alive."

Sheikh Kamel pauses, then resumes:

"Because of spiritual exercise, the internal eye opens. This expression signifies the ability to see, directly what remains hidden from normal eyes. A real Sufi sees things that most people do not. With yet more progress, he will even be able to experience the separation of soul from body. For him, this separation is characterised by a split: while his physical body lies in bed, his double lightly elevates and floats one or two meters above. The physical body does not move; it is left in a state of near total unconsciousness. However, the double knows itself to be the real person who inhabited a moment ago this physical body. The double is a perfect clone. It appears with the same clothing and dimensions as the 'original.' This double is the soul in the astral body, which is of a different nature, subtle and of a particular brilliance. It can pass through walls and fly without wings, like angels (who have wings only in popular imagination!).

When the time of separation comes, consciousness is automatically transferred to the astral double, which is now the only vehicle of the soul: the bird has come out of the cage."

Sheikh Kamel explains more precisely:

"An advanced Sufi doesn't need to die to experience the independence and vast capacities of the soul. He has mastered a specific technique, which he has learned from his master. This technique allows him to leave his body at will and continue, like a free bird, to essential evolution. His goal is to reach the highest state for a soul, to become, so to speak, the great mythic bird that Sufi mythology calls *Simorgh*. This name means 'thirty birds' in Persian.

Sheikh Kamel warns his audience against misunderstanding of the continuation of the travel. He says:

"Those who wait for death, the day the soul leaves the body, should know that physical death does not mean the perfection of the soul or that evolution is complete. Not yet! As explained, physical death is so painless and transparent that the soul does not even notice the difference. Just as when the cage breaks, it generally does not hurt the imprisoned bird. The soul enters the other world, its new residence, in the exact state it was during life on the Earth, neither more nor less developed."

The Sheikh rests, then resumes energetically:

"Be courageous and responsible. You cannot waste opportunities. Use your time fully, the time that remains for the perfecting of the soul to become like a *Simorgh*. You must realise that possessing a physical body is an exceptional occasion for a soul, for development and essential evolution. Evolution towards a higher state should be the real aim of any human soul – the state symbolised by the great *Simorgh* bird. This evolution is the development of the latent faculties of the soul, which yearns for appropriate treatment. It is a refining or purification of the soul.

This corresponds to progressively taking control of animal instincts and drives to give the soul freedom to unfold the divine nature hidden in the deepest part of itself; just as fruit sleeps in a latent and virtual state in the tree and the seed that has been sown yearns to bloom. For each hundred seeds sown in a field, how many will result, after a few years, in strong trees bearing juicy and sweet fruit? It depends on watering, exposure to the sun, protection against insects – in effect, the care the gardener provides. We are responsible for the growth of our internal garden, for our soul, which is our most precious belonging, so that one day it will bear fruit."

Sheikh Kamel develops his speech by this comparison to a gardening work to better reach his audience, made principally of peasant market gardeners. He resumes thus:

"The main work is internal; this specific gardening must be realised during the physical life. The soul, attached to the physical body, is especially favourable to the development of its faculties. The body works somewhat like a greenhouse that allows faster and safer development of fruits.

To avoid mishandling, which could compromise the results, and for a safer and faster evolution, the work must be under the supervision and with the advice of an experienced gardener specialised in the development of the soul. This specialist is a person who knows, for each specific case, the shortest way to the state of the *Simorgh*; he pinpoints the obstacles and helps to overcome them. He is a person who can bring help to seekers on both visible and invisible endeavours."

Sheikh Kamel thus quotes a verse of the Qur'an that says that if a person respects his pact with God, God will do the same. The Sheikh ends his speech thus:

"It is better not to waste time and to get to work on the evolution of the soul. This is the most serious subject matter, because it affects our eternity. Even now we are unconsciously wasting an extraordinary opportunity to 'win our paradise.' Let us get to work so that in a few years the parrot in the cage becomes a *Simorgh*, an immortal and omniscient, brave inhabitant of the spiritual skies."

3 - The Merchant and His parrot

On the third night of the month of Ramadan, Sheikh Kamel recites one of the Masnavi tales to clarify the relationship between body and the soul. Here is the story of the merchant and his parrot[12].

Once upon a time, there was a merchant who had a pretty parrot imprisoned in a cage.

One day as the merchant began to prepare for a trip to India, he asked the parrot, "What do you want me to bring back from the land India?"

To this the parrot replied:

'When you see parrots there, tell them about my situation and say, 'Thanks be to God, there is a parrot who misses you, who is held in my prison. He sends you his greetings, and calls for justice. He asks you to guide and show him the way.'"

And the parrot continued:

"Ask them, 'is it right that I die here, longing for you in separation? Is it right that I remain ruthlessly held, a prisoner, while you enjoy strolling on grass and being in trees? Is this friendship: me in this prison and you in a garden? Remember oh noble friends, this pitiful bird, during your early morning prairies! When a friend remembers a friend, it brings him happiness, more so when one is Leyla and the other Majnoon!'"

---

12 Translated from Masnavi Mirkhani (Tehran, 1331, pp. 42-51), compared to the Masnavi translation, In Search of the Absolute (Paris: Editions du Rocher, 1990).

The merchant agreed to convey this message and to greet any parrot he might encounter.

And so, when the merchant reached the border of India and number of parrots, he stopped his horse, greeted the parrots, and conveyed his parrot's message to them. When the merchant had finished, one of the parrots began to tremble, fell out of the tree and, its breath taken away, died.

The merchant was sorry to have given the message and thought, "I have destroyed this creature. Maybe it was a relative of my little parrot. They must have been one soul in two bodies.

Why did I do this? Why did I bring this message?

I have burned this little creature with my crude words!"

The merchant completed his affairs and happily returned home.

As he arrived back home, the parrot asked, "Where is my gift? Tell me what you saw there and what you said."

"I transmitted your complaint," said he, "to a group of parrots who looked like you. One of them felt your sorrow. It broke his heart and he trembled and died."

When the parrot heard what the other parrot had done, he started to shake violently, fell over and turned cold.

The merchant, seeing his parrot so, fallen and lifeless, leapt up and threw his hat on the floor. And seeing his parrot's colour and condition, the merchant tore open his gown. He cried: 'Oh my beautiful parrot with such a melodious voice, what has happened to you? Why did you die so?

Oh alas, my bird with a soft voice!

Oh alas, my close friend and my confidant!

Oh alas, my melodious bird, wine of my spirit, my garden of paradise!

The Merchant and His parrot

Oh alas, the bird I bought for so little money and whom I have so often neglected!

Oh alas, my light that sets the darkness on fire, my morning that brightens my day!

Oh alas, my bird with such a noble flight, who flies from my end to my beginning!

My parrot, my intelligent bird, interpreter of my thoughts and secrets.

Oh alas, alas, alas, that such a moon is hidden behind the clouds.'

Overcome by the fire of grief and pain, the merchant spoke hundreds of such sentences, his words coloured sometimes with contradictions, sometimes with supplications, sometimes with truth, and sometimes with unreality.

The merchant removed the parrot from the cage and threw him into the air, but only to see the bird take flight and set itself upon a high branch.

He flew as the sun of the Orient invades the sky.

The merchant was amazed. Unconsciously he realised the secret of the parrot.

He looked up at the parrot and said: 'You nightingale! Do me a favour and explain yourself! What did the parrot over there do that has taught you to fool us and cunningly pull the wool over our eyes?'

The parrot answered: 'By his deed, he sent me this message: 'Forget songs, speech and all other openings to people, .for it is your voice that has led to your imprisonment.' He faked his own death to play a trick. He me understand, saying, 'You who has become a musician of the elite and common people, die to find your freedom.'''

Then the parrot delivered, without ill will, one or two words of advice to the merchant, said farewell, and took flight upon these words: "Farewell, you, my owner. You have done me a great favour; you have delivered me from my dark prison. Farewell, you, my owner I am going back to my homeland! I wish that you too be delivered someday, as I am now delivered.'

The merchant said: 'Go, and may God bless you! You have shown me a new way.'

The parrot took the direction of the real India, happy after so much suffering, ordeals, and the grieving.

The merchant thought: 'This advice is for me. I will follow his way, because his way is radiant. How could my soul be lower than a soul of a parrot? This is what the soul must do to become a good example!'

The Symbols

After reciting this tale, Sheikh Kamel takes a deep breath and begins to unravel the symbols of the story:

The merchant represents reason; he travels everywhere for his own interests. He invests only to gain more. He buys something in the East to sell it in the West, and vice-versa. Throughout his life, he is in movement and has an agitated life. He knows no peace.

The cage is the symbol of the elementary body, a prison of the soul. On this subject, Mowlana says:

> *"The body is comparable to a cage; in the praises of those who come and go, it becomes a plague to the soul."*

The parrot represents the soul; he can speak. He can also detach himself from the elementary body and fly in space and time. Mowlana says:

> *"The parrot whose voice is inspired by the divine and whose origin is prior to the origin of existence, this parrot hides in you: it is his reflection that you have seen on the things of the world."*

India is a symbol of the origin of humanity:

"The parrot took the direction of the real India, saying 'Farewell, my owner, I am leaving for my homeland.'"

Sheikh Kamel takes a deep breath, then a sip of hot tea, and again addresses his audience to clarify:

"You must know that parrots, as well as elephants, are two mystic symbols of the soul; both originate from India. India is a huge country. In mystical symbolism, the whole of this territory includes the Orient and the Occident. The earth, its components, as well as the elementary physical bodies, are located in the centre of this country."

The Orient (see the chapter The Two Doors) is the pre-physical world from where the souls come to the material world. The Occident is the world of the post-physical world where all the souls separated from their material skin return.

The tree on which the parrots are sitting symbolises the genealogical tree of humanity.

The death of the parrot is a symbol of detachment and deliverance from egocentrism. Mowlana says:

> *"The meaning of death shown by the parrot is detachment from egocentrism of oneself. In prayer and detachment, let your egocentrism die,*
>
> *So that Jesus' breath reanimates you, making you as beautiful and blessed as he."*

Sheikh Kamel stops suddenly and closes his eyes as if concentrating on his internal world. He raises his head again; his audience is very attentive and still. He decides to say no more on this topic:

"That is all for tonight. I have nothing to add now. Think about it. We will return to this subject some other night but tomorrow I will give you other explanations, God willing, on the visible and invisible worlds."

4 - The Two Worlds (Visible and Invisible)

At the end of the fourth day of the month of Ramadan, Sheikh Kamel, after completing his prayers, begins to develop, as anticipated, a new chapter on the subject of the two worlds. Wearing his simple traditional gown with large sleeves, his hands crossed on his knees, he begins thus:

"In our daily prayers, we speak to God, calling Him *Rabal-alamin*. Which means *God of all universes*. Yet, because of the way our sensory perceptions are tuned, we only know one universe: the material world in which we live. However, there must be many other universes that we cannot perceive with our five senses. Those are the supra-sensible dimensions of our existence."

How is it possible, to explore these hidden dimensions? That is the question. Sheikh Kamel then uses a very concrete image to better impart his message:

"Suppose you are sitting with your friends, watching TV, drinking soda and nibbling pistachios. You are having a lively discussion about the programme you are watching.

Little by little you feel tired. Putting down your glass, you try to stay awake, but your eyelids become heavy, very heavy, as heavy as lead. After a few minutes, you have a very hard time keeping your eyes open. You can still vaguely hear what is being discussed, but then the noise fades away, your eyelids remain closed and sleep overwhelms you. The deeper the sleep, the more your limbs feel numb, as if their activity were slowed down. Now you are cut off from the outside world. You find yourself standing on top of a hill overhanging a very peaceful and deep ocean. There you prepare to dive into the water, a few meters under your feet. A moment later, you are submerged in the blue of the ocean; you dive downwards, leaving behind you layers of water. A beautiful multi-coloured fish swims ahead to guide you to the most hidden corners of the ocean. Schools of shiny fish continually cross your way and waves of vibrations caused by their movements give you a feeling of light massage on your skin. You swim further down away from the surface. You have the sensation that you hang between two layers of water. You do not feel your weight or any gravity hindering you. An unknown source of light illuminates the bottom of the ocean. The deeper you go the more light surrounds you. Your perception of space and time changes every moment…

At this point, your friends, still chattering, turn to you for your opinion on something. They notice that you are absent. They see your closed eyes; you look unconscious. They think: 'He should be left alone, he is sleeping, he perceives nothing, and he is like a dead man…'

But are you really unconscious? Is your link to yourself cut? Of course not! Only the link between you and the outer world is interrupted. Rather, you are totally conscious and in full connection with a parallel world that has a door inside you. The people looking at you have no access to this parallel world and therefore do not understand it. To them such a world cannot exist because their sensory perceptions do not have access to this world. They do not know or see what you are experiencing.

The connection between the human being and his inner world remains permanently established: when awake, asleep, dead, conscious or unconscious. In all situations, only the connection to the outer world is subject to variation.

One of your friends, while putting out a cigarette, knocks the ashtray onto floor; it breaks, producing a tremendous sound. This sudden and sharp noise wakes your sensory perceptions. In a second, you leave the bottom of the ocean of tranquillity where you have been moving and return to the surface of the sensory world. You open your eyes and scrutinise every corner of the living room. For a second, you wonder: 'But where am I? Where are the fish? Who are these people, what do they expect of me?'"

Sheikh Kamel pauses. Stroking his beard, he observes his audience. They are completely absorbed in his words and wait impatiently for him to resume. He says:

"Sleep, in part, resembles death. People watching a dying person perceive only what is sensuously perceptible: they see only an inert body. As a rule, the sleeper does not move, eat, walk, talk, see, or hear, but he does dream. This means that perception does not depend on the activity of the five senses. Sophisticated machines have shown that although the five senses stop functioning during sleep, the activity in some parts of the brain does not stop."

Sheikh Kamel adds:

"The senses connect us to the outer world. During sleep, this connection is cut off, but our consciousness always remains active in a parallel world where time is not defined as in our material world.

Experiences gathered during deep sleep often have a telepathic quality. While the five senses have stopped their activity, the sleeper sometimes sees particular scenes that end up occurring in a few days, weeks, months or years. This confirms that the notion of time changes during deep sleep."

Dream or Reality

After having sipped his fragrant, hot tea, Sheikh Kamel resumes:

"Real Sufis lead a bi-dimensional life. Parallel to their daily social and family engagements, they tend to spiritual matters that connect them to the supra-sensorial universe. This universe is neither imaginary nor virtual, but a real world, just as concrete to its inhabitants as our terrestrial world is to us."

The Beyond

Sheikh Kamel continues:

"Yet the invisible world, or the beyond, is ruled by its own laws, which are different from the physical laws that govern natural phenomena on this Earth. In the supra-sensorial world, imagination is creative, thoughts are tangible realities, and the soul can create its own fantasies and materialize its thoughts. The notions of time and space are different too. But all this require a long explanation. . ."

Sheikh Kamel positively avoids complex discussions. He uses means to simplify difficult aspects of mysticism.

Frankly and very simply, he addresses one of his disciples:

"Let us agree that dream is a reality, even if it is a different reality:

The one who has many material preoccupations remains attracted to the Earth and does not wonder too far from his physical dreaming body. What he sees is in direct relation to his daily life and is, generally, a creation of his own mind.

On the other hand, the one whose mind is at peace and who has little attachment to worldly interests flies far away from his physical body, toward higher heavens, where he may join souls of departed people or even, according to the level of his essential evolution, meet the spirits of wise men and spiritual masters who give him precious teachings and advice.

The brain cells become only partially imprinted with the things of the beyond. On the conscious, level they will only register some symbolic scenes, which later will need interpretation. These interpretations will be very useful advice for right behaviour towards spiritual evolution. You should know that dreams are true barometers that indicate one's state of mind, especially of Sufis. They help the Sheikh to adapt his teaching and advice to the student. The student, in turn, evaluates his own progress, overcomes material and spiritual difficulties to continue on the path to knowledge and spiritual growth. This is why Sufi masters say to their disciples: 'tell me what you dream and I will tell you who you are.' You must know that a Sufi teacher can, through the evaluation of a dream or a vision, 'with the eyes of the soul', discern your real nature, beyond appearances and beyond what you choose to show him.

Sheikh Kamel then begins with the subject of the interpretation of dreams:

"The mystical interpretation of dreams does not belong to psychoanalysis, because the symbolism of dream language has many degrees of complexity. According to the degree in question, some truth remains hidden and inaccessible, protected by access codes known by very few people, as when you have access to a huge amount of information on the Internet, but some sites are protected by access codes.

To the one who knows the language of dreams, much information is contained in visions seemingly deprived of logic; these visions are rich in symbols for the one who holds the key. The interpretation of dreams remains the privilege of very advanced masters. It is also a part of Sufi teachings for the seeker on his spiritual path. He learns the language of dreams and, simultaneously, he learns to know himself. His field of exploration is his own intimate; nature and his personal state of mind.

Therefore, although appearances are sometimes deceptive, it is often in dream that the truth is discovered. But in the world called 'real', each individual can quietly hide his real nature, his real feelings, and his deep motivations."

Raising once again his little glass of tea, Sheikh Kamer examines the attentive audience and finishes his speech for the night with words meant for reflection:

"Where is the truth, dream or reality? The question deserves to be asked."

13 By José Benlliure y Gil (1855–1937): Public domain
http://www.pjvofm.org/75imag/02/1/43.php

5 - The Interpretation of Dreams

Because of the many questions posed by his Sufi students regarding his teachings of the night before - the realm of dreams - Sheikh Kamel decides to deal with the same subject this night.

He begins with these words:

"Those who seek answers to questions about death and the afterlife should pay attention to their dreams. In general, a person spends one third of his life in sleep and is often fascinated by the mystery of this phenomenon.

The Sufi school invites its members to be more aware of their dreams.

Wise men and the followers of the esoteric, who have dealt with very old manuscripts on this subject, have revealed a few secrets concerning the language of dreams and its symbolism. Dreams belong to the mainstream of human culture, but the history of scientific research about sleep is very young. The technological and computerised methods used by scientists have not yet shed much light on this subject.

In Western countries, the cyclical pattern of sleep is studied in special research centres. There, volunteers sleep for an entire week, 24 hours back to back, in dark, soundproof dream laboratories. Researchers, behind two-way mirrors, observe them. Various data are collected in real time on electroencephalographs that register the different stages of sleep, from somnolence to paradoxical sleep, characterized by REM (rapid eye movement). The scientists hope that after analysis of these experiments they will learn more about the functioning of the brain.

A number of such electroencephalographs have shown that there are two distinctive periods to sleep: the slow and rapid period, the latter known as paradoxical. Nowadays, scientists know that, for human beings, sleep is characterised by a loss of consciousness. The activities of bodily functions, the cardiopulmonary and other functions are relatively reduced. Slow sleep occurs in four stages. The first two stages are those of light sleep. The second two represent deep sleep. Stage one is when somnolence, or sleepiness, sets in. Muscles tend to relax gradually, the eye movements slow down, hearing is numbed, and intellectual faculties are particularly reduced. Stage two is that of light sleep, during which muscular activity is totally suspended. Stage three is a transitory phase towards deep sleep. Stage four is the phase of slow, deep sleep, which represents as much as 25% of the complete sleeping time. This corresponds to a span of physical and metabolic healing.

This phase may last longer if the subject has had a full day of physical activity or has had a shortage of sleep. It is difficult to interrupt deep sleep, and if it is sharply interrupted, the subject will feel uneasy in his surroundings and might experience a severe headache. Subsequently, the subject moves to the next period, the paradoxical sleep, which characteristically includes rapid eye movement and a modified cardio-respiratory rhythm, depending on what he sees in dream. The paradoxical sleep lasts about twenty minutes. During this period, the brain is in a state of near consciousness; the subject could awaken at any minute.

The succession of slow and paradoxical sleep lasts about two hours. This cycle will be repeated as many times during the night as the body requires. Even if we cannot control dreams, they are often full of teachings and provide coded messages in a specific language. These messages reflect the present time or the near future, and concern people or events of geographically distant places (yet close mentally, since it is the mental that shows the way to the soul during its nightly excursions). Depending on the nature of his worries and the spiritual dimensions of his soul, the dreamer will be able to connect his soul to the spirits of the dead, to various invisible entities or to spiritual masters, the latter being the best possibility.

In ancient civilizations, dreams served as the main teaching toot for knowledge and comprehension of the world.

Sufism also affords dreams a central place among the tools provided to the seeker, also called *salek*, and his master on the path of spiritual evolution.

On this journey, the disciple receives teachings. He must devote himself to practice a number of exercises: the repetition of *zekr*, prayer or incantations, visualization and concentration on the image of his master, and meditation. Exercise provides the soul with the capacity to approach the other world. Doors open up one after the other. As its vibrations accelerate and its spiritual capacities grow, the soul begins to travel, going ever further out and ever higher up. It experiences things in sleep that are brought back to the conscious level under the form of dreams.

Before rising or turning on the lights, one must immediately and very precisely write down the details of his dreams, because at this time of half-awareness the dreams are still vividly present in the mind. A few minutes later, in a state of complete alertness, the memory of dreams rapidly fades, as if fallen back to inaccessible zones of the memory pushed back by Earthly ideas upon waking.

As soon as possible, the seeker must report his dream to his master and only to him."

Sheikh Kamel warns his listeners not to discuss their dreams. He points out:

"If one narrates his dreams to unqualified persons, his dreams may be interpreted falsely, which may have a negative influence on the materialisation of the dream into reality.

What we see in dream proceeds from a coded language, the knowledge of which is the privilege of those who have carried out and concluded the journey of the soul. These are the masters, the real mystics, who possess the key to the interpretation of dreams.

The master adapts his teachings to what the disciple sees in dream. He may give his disciple a new *zekr*, add or decrease exercises, give him indications of how to lead his life, how to avoid dangers, or how to help his fellow humans in difficulty.

The master teaches his disciple by the disciple's dreams, which he completes and confirms with his own vision."

Sheikh Kamel suddenly stops, as if to make sure that each person understands every word of his speech. After a long lapse or meditative silence, he continues slowly:

"You must know that the lonesome seeker, the one who goes his own way, without a teacher or guide, can hardly get very far.

Of course, he may practice techniques found in books, but he has very little chance to find by himself, the appropriate *zekr* or to change the *zekr* at the appropriate time, because he is not capable of interpreting his own dreams, unless he is already a master!

The master is not only a trainer, but a translator, as well."

To conclude, Sheikh Kamel quotes from the Shahnameh, or The Book of Kings, the Old Persian epic, where dreams are provided, privileged place. He carefully explains how decisions seem to be taken chiefly on the basis of dreams and their interpretation, rather basis of external, worldly manifestations. Epic heroes mainly seek through their dreams: they seek their kings, guides, spouses, war or reconciliation. Surprisingly, in an epic, at least twenty dreams are mentioned and commented upon, followed by the narration of their materialisation in the physical world. There are cases where two opponents dream the same dream concerning a third person. They try to influence reality to their own interests based on what they have seen in dream; but in the end they realise that there is no way to change the course of the story already contemplated in the world of dream.

6 - The Old Wandering Musician

On this night, Sheikh Kamel wishes to resume his speech on the importance of dreams. He recites on the tales of the Masnavi[14]:

"Once upon a time there was an old solitary musician who travelled from one place to the other, living off the generosity of the people who appreciated his music. He played the harp and sang traditional melodies that brought joy to the hearts of the villagers. Our troubadour was a good man, his heart was pure and he was happy to exercise his art.

In those times, Omar, second caliph of Islam, ruled the entire Muslim world. He enforced a very strict and dogmatic version of the religion, hating whatever was joyful, especially music.

Our old musician was tired from so many long years of wandering. His old fashioned music, along with his weakened voice, did not attract the public any longer, and people began to show indifference to his art. He fell into disgrace.

One day he entered the city of Medina, capital of Islam and seat of the Caliph Omar, and the public did not even allow him to complete his repertoire. They chased him away, beyond the city walls. He was desperate and did not know what to do. He went to a cemetery and sat on a very old gravestone, riddled and broken through the years. He laid his head in his hands and cried:

'Oh God, I have been playing music my whole life, going from place to place, and now that I have grown old, people do not want me anymore. I am lonesome and a stranger: here. What can I do now that no one wants to hear my music? I am

---

14 Mirkhani, vol. 1, p.51

going to sing for You!' Taking his harp, he sang all the songs of his repertoire until he was so exhausted that he fell asleep.

He slept and the bird of his soul escaped its prison: leaving behind the musician and his instrument.

It set itself free: Thus, it was set free from the body and free from the tortures of the world;

Roaming in the universe of tranquillity, in the middle of a spiritual landscape;

His soul in that world said: If they would leave me as I please in this surrounding I would look all around, without needing eyes I would pick roses and flowers, without using hand. I would travel all over, without needing feet or wings; I would eat sweets, without needing a mouth or teeth, I would sit in Zekr and Fekr sessions with the inhabitants of yonder, without being subject to headaches and worries.

Because this earth and these skies, in spite of their immensity, are so narrow; that they have torn my heart in sorrow.

Yet, the world they have shown to me has opened my eyes to its greatness; if that world and the way to it were accessible, not one second would anyone remain here.

During this time Caliph Omar was busy ruling his kingdom. As he was on his throne in the middle of an audience, he felt an urge to sleep. He felt numb, closed his eyes, and had a strange dream. He saw a majestic, luminous person, who came to him and instructed him to gather, hundred gold coins, to take them to the cemetery for a friend of God. 'He has served us well, you must pay him.'

Closing his eyes, carried off by sleep, he had a dream. A voice came to him from God and his soul heard it.

He heard a voice that is at the origin of all sounds and vibrations.

This is the true voice and everything else is mere noise, The Kurds, the Turks, as well as those who speak Persian, and the Arabs, they all indifferently understand this voice without ears or mouth.

What does it say Turks, Tadjiks and Africans and even wood and stones understand what this voice says.

Omar awoke very impressed by the scene he had dreamed. He gave Instructions to his treasurer to fetch 100 gold coins and-to meet him at the cemetery. He went to the cemetery to look for God's friend to fulfil his assignment. But he saw no one, except an old musician asleep on a broken old gravestone.

Omar, who hated music, went back to the city, without having found God's friend. He resumed his affairs of the kingdom. Hardly had he begun to receive his subjects in audience that he once again felt numb, as he had that morning. He closed his eyes and saw the same dream as before. Frightened, Omar rushed to the cemetery. Once again, he found only the old musician, to whom he now gave the bag full of gold coins. He then returned to his palace."

Common Language or Collective Memory?

We cannot help but notice that long before the birth of Jungian psychoanalysis, Mowlana had spoken of language known to all humanity, people of all races and cultures, all civilizations: a common or original language known even to the subatomic particles constituting the natural elements. This language which comes through dreams from the supra-sensible world is inaudible. One hears it directly in the head; it does not cause vibration in the inner ear[15].

---

15 When we visited the Toulouse microwaves laboratory, I asked Mr Thourel, now retired:

In this story, Mowlana raises a question:

"The prophets also have some internal notes that provide priceless life for those who are in search of it.

The sensuous ear does not hear these notes, because it is soiled by sin. The voice of the jinn [peri] is not perceived by man, because he is incapable of understanding the mysteries of jinn [peri]. Although the

---

"Do you think that the brain's organ behave like receptors of high frequency electromagnetic waves modulated in low frequency?"

"Yes I think so," he responded. "A few years ago, we preformed tests with radar waves in very high frequencies, modulated on the frequency of 500 Hz. When our heads cross or intercept the radar beam, we could perceive a very clear whistle, corresponding to the modulation frequency. We had to be very careful, because the effects of these radar waves on the human tissues are not well known. There have been very serious accidents, including death, around very powerful radars."

"In other words," I said, "this sound signal was perceived directly inside the head of the subject without any sound propagation?"

"Exactly, and as these beams are directional, one could have aimed with an antenna at the head of a person and have produced a sound in his head, without other people around him noticing"

I said: "If one could modulate these radar waves with a pure frequency corresponding to a sound of constant value, nothing prevents us from imagining a modulation with a complex sound even with the human word?"

"This is a fact"

I said: "In other words, with such a system, which technically is not particularly difficult, it would be possible to speak to a person lost in a mass of people, and talk 'in his head' without people around him perceiving the message" "What we are sure of is that microwaves have an action on the nervous system. More generally expressed, such a radiation can bring only a state of physical shock on the subject, adding to the evident psychological shock, and can be accompanied by a state of drowsiness until the nervous system returns to its normal state ((Travel to the Boundaries of Science - An Investigation on UFOS, Jean Pierre Petit, Arbin Micher, 1992 pp. 144-146).

voice jinn [peri] also belongs to this world, the voice of the heart is louder.

The internal notes of the saints say, first, 'Oh you, particles of the nonexistence,

Take heed, raise your head out of the "*lā*" of negation, and give up this useless imagination.'

If you speak any of these notes, the souls will rise up from the graves. Bring your ear close, for this melody is not far, but it is not permitted to communicate it to you.

They say:

"This voice is distinct from all voices; resurrection of the dead is the deed of God's voice."

As having fallen into a slumber, and after having experienced this somehow different form of dream, Omar came to himself, he felt that the situation was unusual."

Sheikh Kamel stops to be sure his audience follows him. Then he resumes:

"The lesson of this story is that when we do something with humility for God, God hears and rewards us. As long as we do not feel lonely and trapped, God will not manifest Himself. But when there is no solution, and the only way, is to seek God's grace, God is present to help us.

Human reason is essentially based on the law of causality. For each cause there is an effect, and for each problem we try to find a logical solution. Also, each effect results from a cause. The human being is limited in mind by this rational linearity. Thus, anytime we find no logical solution we become desperate. We forget that the universe is governed by other laws than the simple law of causality; for instance, the law of serial, which escapes our logic. We attribute it to chance, which is only a way to designate the laws that we do not know.

Let us take the case of a closed room with one door and one window. In principle, we can get out of the room only through the door. If we do not have the key to this do, we try to get out through the window. First, we try to open the window, and then, if it too is locked, we break the windowpane.

If the windowpane is armoured, and one cannot break it, there is no logical exit out of the room. Next we will knock on the walls to see if there is a weak spot, or to be heard outside and to be saved. Then we will lose patience and lose hope of being rescued. If we stick to logic, we will fall into despair. But if we believe in other super-rational laws, which connect us to the supra-sensory world, we will not lose hope. We will pray and ask God for help, and wait for the situation to change to our favour in an unexpected, irrational way that, for example, a trapdoor opens in the ceiling and a rope drops to help us. This is not luck, but the interference of other laws at work in our universe.

Those who believe in God and in the supra-sensory world also believe in active interventions between that world and ours. This is demonstrated by the story of the Prophet Joseph in the holy texts of the Bible and Qur'an, in the Masnavi texts of Mowlana, and also in the stories of *Bijan* and *Key-Khosrow* in the *Shahnameh* (Book of Kings) of Ferdowsi."

7 - The Post-Physical World

On the seventh night of the month of Ramadan, Sheikh Kamel continues to address the subject of the previous two nights. He wants to bring his audience closer to the unexplored zones of the supra-sensuous universe. First, he attentively observes the faces of the people sitting in a circle around him. He wants to be sure that they are ready to receive his message. He says:

"We have already spoken about a world that comes after ours; the world to which the soul goes after leaving the body. Occultists, magi, and other would-be spiritualists call it by different names, such as the astral, or, intermediary world, Catholics call it Purgatory, Buddhists call it Bardo, and other religions call it "the Beyond." It is a world inhabited by spirits, jinn, fairies, and devils. It is principally the world of the dead, where each of us will go after physical death.

The astral world is in fact composed of many plains vibrating on various frequencies. These plains are stacked on top of one another, on a vibratory scale. On this scale, the low vibrations of the lower astral are situated immediately next to our world in an area inhabited by numerous jinn and other not very recommendable creatures. On the level of high vibrations of the higher astral dwell developed spirits who are about to move to the unlimited spiritual world, which in turn leads to the divinity.

The astral world is as real for its inhabitants as the physical world is to us. The laws ruling that world are somewhat different from the ones we are used to. For example, time does not exist in the astral world; one second is like 1000 years on Earth. Through Einstein's theory of relativity, we know that time is subjective. The astral world also ignores the idea of distances, because in that world, the mind has a power and reality is foreign to us. In the beyond, it is enough to think about someone for that person then to be facing you. You have only to think about something and it materialises before your eyes.

When we mention the eyes, we mean of course the eyes of the astral body!

Indeed, in addition to the physical body, each of us has an invisible astral body, also called a soul. During our Earthly life, this astral body is on top of our physical body. It will come off when we die and go into the astral world to live its own life. The astral body also has five senses, adapted to the world where the soul dwells. These astral senses, when they are well developed during the physical life, are called the sixth sense and are responsible for the visions and intuitions of clairvoyants; for example, the voices heard by Joan of Arc, to cite one famous example. From here on, we will use the word soul instead of astral body or energetic body, because they all mean the same. During our lifetime on Earth, we often neglect our soul, because we are unaware of its existence. In fact, the soul expresses itself only in dreams. Dreams are the memories transferred from the soul to the brain when it, the soul, returns to the body after an astral journey. The soul travels in the invisible world while the physical body restores its strength in sleep and gathers energy after an active day.

But we are wrong to neglect our soul!

We are wrong because the soul is our real residence, the vehicle that we keep after death. It is the only thing we can take with us behind the veil when we leave our body that has become useless, as when we leave a broken and useless car on the side of the road.

There is in each of us a door to the astral or post-physical world.

This door can be opened and crossed both ways during Earthly life, especially in the dream phase, when we sleep, or during hypnosis or meditation. After death, this door closes forever, when the soul has left the physical body it is rendered forever useless.

Every night we open this door unconsciously when we dream. We open it one last time when we die. Our death corresponds to our definitive entry into the astral world. Our evolution continues on the other side, in a place corresponding to our capacity and nature. The rougher our soul and the more materialistic our aspirations, the lower we remain, very close to the physical world. A number of deceased people never really leave our world. They roam during a time, which corresponds to many hundreds of years for us, around the significant places of their past existence; they are wretched ghosts, still attracted by the things of this world. They practically haunt their earlier homes.

Others will rise to various plains where their learning and evolution will continue, where they will make themselves useful. Other creatures will sink into dense plains, crowded with diabolical and criminal creatures, to whom they are similar: those who resemble, assemble."

What about Reincarnation?

Sheikh Kamel looks thoughtful, maybe a little worried. He decides to warn the people against a wrong interpretation of the one-way journey of the soul towards its supra-sensible residence. He strokes his grey beard, and then resumes his explanations:

"Keep in mind that as soon as the soul leaves this material world, there is no possible return. This is the reason why the notion of reincarnation is excluded from all monotheistic religions. What the holy books mention is in fact resurrection. But there is in every religion a contradictory debate among its theologians about resurrection. Some think that on the Day of Judgment, God will destroy all universes and immediately recreate them the following moment. Thus all souls will return to their elementary bodies as reward for their past deeds. Other theologians maintain that resurrection has nothing to do with the soul's return to the elementary body, but that it is rather a return to the subtle non-material body. The guardians of the temples in Pharaonic Egypt write in The Book of the Dead that there will be a resurrection at the end of time. With this prospect in mind, mummification was practiced to allow the soul an easy return to its bodily residence. Yet, in hieroglyphic texts, as well on bas-relief carvings of the ancient Egyptians, the journey of the soul leaving its dead body is one way."

Sheikh Kamel mentions Sumerian scripts, written nearly 7000 years ago, describing, through the adventures of Gilgamesh and his friend Ankidoo, the travels of the soul in the world of the dead. The Sheikh says:

"Here again we see that Babylonian wise men attest to the journey of the soul after death as a one-way journey and that the soul can never return to Earth to re-enter a new elementary body. The origins of the reincarnation argument are to be found in very old times, perhaps as early as the Neanderthal era, at the beginning of humankind. In most primitive tribes studied by our researchers, this very old belief still persists. Pre-historical man believed that the soul of a dead person does not leave this world, but that it spreads to trees, stones, and animals, and even impregnates new-born babies or other living persons. The Australian aborigines still believe this. It is a primitive belief that belongs to primitive populations. In India this has resulted in another vision of the world. Nirvana, which made it possible for the Karma to escape forever the cycle of rebirth, Samsara, represents a transition of this archaic vision of the world towards developed mysticism.

Out of their esoteric contemplations, the mystics have brought us reliable information concerning post-physical worlds.

The Tibetan Book of The Dead, or *Bardo Thodol* describes the journey of the soul after death. In spite of a general conviction, this introductory book, written by lamas, does not describe an immediate and systematic reincarnation, but a journey of the soul in what is called The Six Worlds Of Impermanence. This corresponds to the physical world as well as to the astral plains inhabited by spirits, angels, demons and many other creatures."

Sheikh Kamel stops to sip his fragrant tea. He then addresses audience with more energy:

Reincarnation or the return of the soul to a new physical world is a theory resulting from the shaman and lama experiences.

After long ascetic and esoteric practices, they become capable of entering a sort of trance or hypnotic state, which allows them to exit their physical body, the way each one of us does during deep meditation. Then they can travel more or less voluntarily in parallel landscapes that are in direct contact with our sensible world.

During trance, the relationship to objects is very different from what we know. In other words, there is direct knowledge: the contemplation of an object is equal to unity with that object. Distance is abolished and the contemplator unites with the object of contemplation. He feels this from inside, and experiences reality without alterations based on the sensuous organs, as occurs in our physical world.

Thus a lama in deep meditation, contemplating someone, identifies himself with that person. Inside himself he feels the experiences and the personality of that person; he feels himself becoming that person.

Therefore, when he comes back to himself after meditation, he is sure of having been this person.

It is very easy to assimilate this practice to the theory of reincarnation. The astral experiences, lived by the soul outside of the physical body, are mixed with the past astral experiences, lived in this world, and one concludes having lived other lives before this life.

In the world of the soul, time does not exist. Past events are lined up next to the most recent events, without any chronological order.

Thus, in the astral world, when you unconsciously think about a historical period, you find yourself projected in that period. The events taking place there will be lived in someone's body with whom we identify during the whole process of contemplation. When we return from this vision, we naturally believe to have lived those scenes in a preceding life, very long ago. Yet all this happened in a parallel world, out of space and time."

At this point, Sheikh Kamel wants to emphasise his message. He uses a more scientific language:

"Theoretically, we can use very powerful telescopes and modern astronomical tools to observe space at the first moments of creation. According to Einstein's theory, because light moves at a known speed, if we could move faster than light, we could turn back time!

The soul is capable of such a deed; its field of investigation includes the past as well as the future.

Some populations have even developed the theory of metempsychosis, the theory of reincarnation as a plant or animal. In a state of deep meditation, during the 'time' spent in the visible world, it is possible to identify with a vegetal or animal.

Yet, supporters of the theory of systematic reincarnation argue that there have been many cases of small children telling their shocked parents about their previous lives. It has often been possible to verify the veracity of these stories.

Also, the choice of the *Tuklus* of Tibet, the young children picked out as reincarnation of recently deceased lamas, requires very precise criteria. The child must be able to select personal objects that belong to the old master. Then other lamas receive confirmation of the *Tuklu* through dreams and meditative visions.

There is however very little known phenomenon called 'connection,' which is, often confused with reincarnation, but which follows another logic.

Thus a spirit can connect to the soul of a newborn baby through the power of spiritual attraction. This happens because he needs to complete his own evolution by experiencing the Earthly life of that child, or to fulfil a spiritual mission he could not complete during his own Earthly life. The second case concerns, of course, the Tibetan *Tuklus*.

Incidentally the connection may be occasional, for a relative length of time depending on the needs, or it may be permanent.

This is not real incarnation, because the physical person to whom the spirit connects has his own soul. The free spirit simply enters in connection with the soul of its host through the power of spiritual attraction. If it's a bad spirit, it is a case of possession, as the popular definition goes."

The Dangers Of Idealising Reincarnation

Sheikh Kamel takes a break. The subject has been dense, but is not yet finished. Some details must be clarified. The Sheikh speaks:

"The great Sufi masters, such as Sheikh Ala-Odoleh of Semnan, around the year 700 of the Hegira, have very firmly and without hesitation criticised belief in reincarnation as a vision of the world. According to the masters, this point of view is the result of a false interpretation of the contemplated parallel world. They were correct, because such a vision of the world can become pillars of an active ideology, replacing in many circles some old fashioned ideologies such as Marxist-Leninism. This philosophy may produce drifts towards negative effects. With this philosophy, the follower may adopt various positions. He may resign himself to his sad situation, on the grounds that he is purging bad karma accumulated during previous lives. This point of view not only justifies the caste system as practiced in India, but also slavery.

Or he may consider himself as having the right to do anything he pleases, including the worst excesses, since he can make up for it later, in a future life. In ancient China, where reincarnation was recognised by all, there were cases in which people acquired debts to be repaid in the next life!

Such an attitude can lead, within a few generations, to total decadence of a civilisation.

This vision of the world is very old. In some primitive, very materialistic civilisations, people lived with the hope of returning after their death, to continue to take advantage of worldly goods.

No Sufi text supports the theory of reincarnation. Many masters, such as Mullah Sadra, Mohy-Edin Arabi, Sohrevardi, Nassir-Edin Tussi,

Avicenna, explain the laws that govern birth, life on Earth, and death. They refer to the continuity of the journey of the soul after death. According to these sources, after death, each individual remains at the stage where his soul was during his physical life. However, he will be able to develop and progress if he is in contact with a superior spirit who has enough spiritual power to draw him up, towards higher vibrations."

The One-Way Of The Two Doors

Sheikh Kamel proposes a comparison – the one-way flow of blood in the heart cavities. Then he returns to the main subject:

"According to these texts, the material world is one way with two doors. One door, coming from the pre-physical world, is the entrance, and the other door to the post-physical world, is the exit. Between these two doors, the evolution of the soul is a one-way transformation. Spiritual energy flows in a one-way channel, under the forces of the invisible world, without ever returning to the source, just like a stream where water never flows backwards. The post-physical world is very vast, made of various plains that never cross one another and that are stacked one on top of the other, on different wavelengths. This is similar to TV channels or stories of a building. Jesus said, 'My Father's Kingdom has many mansions.'

At the time of death, there are three possible situations, according to the soul's density for the deceased: If the soul is very dense and heavy with much rough and egoistical attraction to material things of life, it will be attracted downwards, towards lower astral worlds, commonly called hell, just like a pebble sinks in the ocean.

If the soul is particularly light, almost liberated from animal impulses, it will be attracted upwards, towards higher vibrations, by the electromagnetic forces of the invisible world like a balloon flying in the sky.

A middle soul, neither too heavy nor too light, neither very materialist nor very spiritual, which is the case with most of us, will stay close to the Earth and to the vibrations of this world for an indefinite time; it will float like an empty bottle on the ocean and roam around like a sad soul until it somehow grows under the influence of other spirits trying to help it realise its situation and the possibilities open to it."

8 - The Pre-Physical World

It is the eighth night and the Sheikh prepares to resume his teachings. He wants to say everything, within the capabilities and learning capacities of each member of his audience. This night is dedicated to explanations of the pre-physical world. He begins thus:

"In opposition to the post-physical world, which is enriched with diverse existences and evolutions of all creatures inhabiting that world, the pre-physical world is of a very different nature. It is a world of potentialities in the simple state of existence, in a state of latency before their manifestation in the physical world.

This world is like a source of the clearest and purest water. When they move to the material world, these elements become complex. Their potential is activated, just like a seed, in spite of its apparent simplicity, and contains all the potential characteristics of the tree it can become if it is properly exposed to sunlight, regularly watered, and protected from insects.

Let us elaborate on this analogy: when a tree burns or dematerializes into carbon, it reaches the last stage of its evolution on Earth. Meanwhile, its invisible counterpart moves to the post-physical world, just like the soul that leaves the physical body upon death.

This pre-physical world may be considered the centre of creation, the starting point of light. When light reaches the tree, photosynthesis occurs, the tree evolves. The tree will never become seed again; its evolution is irreversible. The same is true for human beings.

This pre-physical world possesses a one-way door opening to the material world where develop as physical bodies."

The Broken Taboo

The Sheikh stops. He feels he has said everything about the journey of the soul through the three layers of existence. But instead of concluding, he begins a new discussion, as though he wished to bring the audience to attention.

"The consideration of the soul and questions relating to death have progressed a great deal over the centuries. In ancient Egypt, for instance, death was a part of people's daily lives. East of the river Nile was the city of the living, and the necropolis, the city of the dead, was west of the river Nile, on the side of the setting sun. There were ceremonies, suggesting the transition of the soul from the physical world to the invisible world, and this was symbolised by crossing the Nile in a small boat. Many hieroglyphs show the journey of the soul after death. The subjects of death and the soul were not considered to be taboos, as there are today. On the contrary, death was considered as one of the main stages of life and every person prepared for it according to the recommendations and teachings of the priests of that time, who were experts of the occult.

Nowadays, in contrast, death has no place in life. Any reminder of the "great crossing" has been carefully erased or kept hidden so that nothing in daily life brings the subject of death to mind. And when we are brought to think about death, all we see is absolute darkness, and this darkness is what frightens us.

When the inevitable moment comes, everybody is destabilised, because no one is prepared for the journey of the soul. The one who dies finds himself in a situation similar to the one who must go out in winter but has no adequate clothing for the season; he suffers and is distressed. Also, those who remain behind suffer, because they have not been prepared to confront this situation. For them, separation is distressing, and they have no hope of ever seeing the deceased again.

It is not a question of believing or not believing in the survival of the soul: those who cannot see the invisible do not want to hear or accept what the mystic's say, those who are capable of going, at will, to the other world. Their logic is: 'I have no eyes; therefore I do not want to open my ears.' That's a strange logic!

Yet every morning, before going out, everyone listens to the weather forecast (even if the national weather forecast is wrong every other day). Sometimes we open the window to get an idea of the weather, before wearing the appropriate clothes. But when it comes to questions of the other world, the beyond, and to the conditions we are going to find there, nobody cares to know, as if there were no way to find out.

People behave as if they were to live on this Earth for the next 100,000; they make absolutely no preparations for their eternity.

What will they do when confronted with reality?"

9 - Escaping Death

On the ninth night of the month of Ramadan Sheikh Kamer recites one of the Masnavi [16] tales concerning those who do not want to accept the reality of things:

One day a man came to Solomon, pale with anxiety.

Solomon asks him, "What is it?"

The man said; "Today Azraiil (the Archangel of death) has given me a bad look, full of hatred."

Solomon asked: "What do you want?

The man said: "Tell the wind to carry me to India."

Solomon ordered the wind to carry the man immediately to India. The next day, the Angel came to visit Solomon, who asked him, "Is it true that you have given that Muslim a look full of wrath?"

The Archangel answered, "I was stupefied as I passed by him. God had commanded me to take his soul that day in India! Then I thought, "even if he had hundred wings, how could he ever get there?"

After having told this story, sheikh Kamel begins to talk about suicide.

Suicide

"The Prophet of Islam said: 'Die before death takes you away'[17]. According to theologians, interpreters and mystics, this sentence

---

16 (Ed. Mirkhani, vol. 1, p.26.)

17 Hadith cited by Muslim and Bakri and Sanaii/Divan Qassayed.

alludes to the principle of essential evolution. Because the human being is a creature who develops and surpasses itself, he is the only animal capable of controlling its instinctive drives to allow his spirit to move towards perfection. In fact, the human being is composed of an existence and an essence. The latter is an evolving reality. At any moment an individual may become a devil or an angel.

He becomes a devil if the demonic drives in him dominate. He becomes an angel if the angelic attributes of his soul dominate. Between angel and devil, the fight stops only when one or the other has won. This perpetual fight is symbolised by the combat between an eagle and a dragon. False interpretations expressed by people who were not qualified to comment on sacred texts have caused much confusion about this hadith. Muhammad's words, 'Die before death takes you away,' and Moses' words, 'Return to God and kill your nafs (ego),' do not encourage suicide, but perfection. Suicide is hateful to God and his prophets, because through suicide, we definitively stop the evolution of our essence. The Qur'an explicitly condemns suicide:

"Do not take risks that endanger your life"[18].

To preserve your life and the life of others is the highest responsibility of the human being. The one who commits suicide kills an individual: himself. The Qur'an says: *"Killing one single person is equivalent to annihilating all of humanity, and giving life to someone is to save the life of the whole humanity*[19]*."*

---

18 Surah 2, v: 195.

19 Surah 5, v: 32.

10 - Reality and Illusion

Sheikh Kamel seems satisfied with the results of his teachings up to now. The Sufis have asked thoughtful questions, showing how concerned they are with such matters. Tonight, he decides to raise a new subject: reality and illusion, complementary to but independent from subjects of the previous nights. Let us hear what he has to say:

"We perceive the world through our five senses, which send information to our brain. Using an internal logic specific to the cerebral system, the brain translates these sensory facts. Using imagination, it then turns to memory to complete or modify a seemingly incomplete or illusory piece of information.

The frontal cortex assembles the whole of the information perceived by the five senses. The assembled, incoming elements represent our perception of the world. This frontal cortex feeds our abilities of comprehension.

In other words, our understanding of the world that surrounds us is not of an outside reality, but of an interpretation of that world by our brain.

This is how a magician can fool thousands of spectators who will swear, in good faith, to have seen something incredible. In effect, they have perceived something incredible, but it is not objective reality. An experienced magician knows how to use and manipulate the internal logic of our brain. He does it without our knowing and to his own advantage. This is the secret of his art, in addition to long and advanced training.

Because our conscious tools of perception (the five senses and the brain) are not reliable, we are never sure about interpreting information coming in from the external world correctly. Sometimes this information creates an illusion of reality, as perceived by the five senses.

On this subject, I would now like to tell you three tales by Mowlana:

The Shadow and the Bird

A bird flew in the sunny sky, projecting its shadow on the ground.

The villagers who never looked up and who were used to scrutinizing the ground saw the bird's shadow mistaking it with the real bird, throwing arrows at it, without success!

Here, the ground symbolises the sensuous world, here on Earth, and the arrows represent the mind oriented towards what it takes to be reality, but which in truth is just a shadow. People aim at the wrong target, because reality is above, like the bird; it is supra-sensorial.

The more we concentrate on the ground, that is, on the sensorial world, the further away we move from the truth above. We are overwhelmed with illusions produced by this world.

Using the principle of negation, it is possible to bring down the curtain of the sensuous world, so as to contemplate the reality of each being in its actual state.

Here are two more stories showing how much we can be fooled by our mental imagination, which makes no difference between illusion and reality.

The Deluded Cuckold

Once upon a time there was a woman who had a lover she could never meet because her husband was always around. Thus she decided to fool her husband: she took her to a fruit tree and climbed the tree, under the pretext of picking fruit. After having picked two or three fruits, she looked down.

She screamed at the poor, dumbfounded man, 'What are you doing with this woman! What shame! Stop now!' The poor man protested; he had been waiting for her, like a good man, at the foot of the tree! She was in a rage, as if she had really seen her husband making love to another woman.

She descended and suggested that he climb the tree. He did so. At this moment, the came and the poor cuckold, sitting in the tree, could observe how his wife and the man made love. Leaning on a branch and shaking his head, the poor man shouted to his very busy wife: 'You were right, this is a strange tree. It causes hallucinations!'

This short tale again illustrates the same idea: in the world of illusions, which our mind and imagination create in front of our eyes, there is often confusion between what really happens and what we apprehend, what we think is going on.

Our comprehension of the world does not always correspond to real events. We mistake illusion for reality and sometimes reality for illusion, like our poor cuckold!

We cannot capture and understand for sure the realities of this world with the five physical senses. More so, we cannot perceive the realities of the supra-sensuous world without the sixth-sense, which gives us direct knowledge. The sixth sense makes it possible because it bypasses normal senses and reason, which is the source of our illusions.

The Influenced Professor

Once upon a time there was a very strict professor. A group of his students had decided to get rid of him, using an original trick:

Before the beginning of class, one student came close to the professor, looked at him with concern and said, "Are you ill? Your skin is yellow and your eyes are red. You must have something!" Our professor firmly answered that he felt perfectly healthy. Then a second student arrived who looked sincerely worried and asked, "You look funny this morning. Do you feel well, Professor?" "Uh, I don't feel anything special," said the professor, a little uncertain. A few minutes later, as he was about to start his class, a third student came forward and added, "Sir you are very pale and your eyes are swollen, what has happened?"

The professor became convinced that he did not feel well. He telephoned his wife, telling her to call the doctor, and then he went home. When the doctor came, he was prostrated in a corner, nauseated and with a bad headache.

This short tale shows that even health, our inner-truth, can be affected by deceptions and illusions of the outer world that we perceive through the five senses. Our self-confidence may be altered, and we are no longer able to distinguish between illusion and reality – even with what concerns our health. What can we then say about outer manifestations and the world surrounding us?

What reliable tools do we have to understand what is going on around us in the physical world? Similarly, how can we understand what is going on in the other world, the metaphysical world, which, somehow 'surrounds from inside' the physical world, upon which it is superimposed?

The goal of Sufism is to develop these tools within each of us: this sixth sense that leads to the truth by way of direct, non-verbal knowledge is beyond the limited and unreliable five senses.

By such tales, through the principle of negation, Mowlana wants to question our partial and false knowledge, which is not adequate for total understanding of the reality.

On this subject, Mowlana gives us another tale:

The Elephant in the Dark

One night in a mountain village, just after sunset, came an unknown traveller with a huge animal unknown to the villagers. The man was Indian and his mount, a magnificent elephant.

The traveller took a room at the inn. He also asked for a stable for his travel companion. The news that a stranger with a strange animal had come to the village spread very rapidly throughout the tavern; no one had seen the stranger and his animal, it being dark outside and there not being enough candles.

The people speculated on the real nature of this unknown animal. Their curiosity was so strong that three of them crossed the yard, opened the door halfway, and snuck into the stable where the elephant rested in complete darkness.

After hesitating, the first man held out his hand, which slid on the tusk, down to its tip. His imagination did the rest of the work. Our man ran out proclaiming out loud that the animal is a sort of bovine, since it has big, smooth and pointed horns.

The second man carefully went along the wall to the other end of the stable. He held out his hand and took hold of the tail, which was short, narrow and with a brush of thick hair, like the tail of a camel. This was enough for our brave villager who went happily to his fellows, declaring that the animal was most probably a cousin of the camel, an animal very well known in those regions.

The third man, not so brave, remained at the door, went down on his hands and knees, and searched over the ground with his hand. He brushed against the moist and flexible trunk of the thick-skinned animal, which was exploring the paved ground of the stable in search of straw twigs. For this man it was clear that the animal was a huge serpent.

Raising their voices in argument, each of the three men was convinced of the truth, having personally touched the animal. The owner of the tavern decided to mediate an agreement. From under his counter he pulled out a magnificent candle. Together with the three villagers who were curious and very much sure of themselves, they crossed the yard. What a surprise as the man held up the candle and brought light to the stable. They could see the totality of the elephant. This put an end to the interpretations produced by each man's imagination."

Figure 4- The Central Mehrab in Mosque–Cathedral of Córdoba, Spain

11 - Meditation

On this night, Sheikh Kamel wishes to draw conclusion from the stories he told last night. He first explains that direct knowledge of objects, phenomenon, and beings of this world is not possible so long as we perceive by our five senses only. Without direct knowledge, we cannot be certain of our convictions resulting from our researches. He says that the human being has three ways of achieving supra-sensory knowledge:

(1) Death; (2) Sleep; and (3) Meditation.

He gives his disciple a few minutes to internalise this message, and then resumes his discussion of the three paths:

"Physical death marks a definitive extinction of the five physical senses. After death, the soul goes through interesting experiences, sometimes told by those who have come back to life (near death experiences, NDE), after having come close to the great departure. The soul generally has no control over its own journey.

Sleep that naturally leads to dream awareness leaves only fragments of memory upon awakening, when returning to the state of normal awareness. During sleep, the wandering in the parallel world depends on many factors, among them how deep the sleep is. However, neither the direction nor the orientation of the spirit can be controlled.

Deep meditation represents the only means of voluntary immersion in the supra-sensible world. Meditation allows us to reach this state of trans-awareness, so difficult to describe in words. In opposition to death and sleep, meditation allows each person to move from the conscious world to the supra-sensible world and to travel there in a voluntary and conscious way.

The fundamental difference between dreaming and meditating is that during sleep, the journey of the soul is uncontrollable. The soul goes where its vibration frequency and the magnetic currents carry it. But in a state of meditation, it is possible to control and direct the astral journey.

During physical life, when the soul is linked to a body, one who knows the appropriate techniques can travel between both worlds; not only in the post-physical and pre-physical worlds, but in the past and future, as well. After death, the door to the pre-physical world is definitively closed to the disembodied soul.

Meditation is the shortest way to the supra-sensible world. Because the five senses cease to function during meditation, it is considered a voluntary death. This has nothing to do with the biological meaning of the word 'death.' Meditation is the key to the separation of soul and body. No one who is sensuously aware can roam around the supra-sensible world. The passage from the sensible world to the supra-sensible world happens when the five senses have been blocked. This happens generally during a quarantine in which the person uses concentration techniques, alone in a solitary place, far from noise and light.[20]

> *'Turn your face to the wall of solitude*
>
> *Take retreat from all, even from yourself*
>
> *The clever takes retreat at the bottom of a well*
>
> *Because the heart cleans itself in seclusion.'"*

---

20 Mowlana Masnavi, Mirkhani, vol. 1, p.35.

After quoting this passage of Masnavi, Sheikh Kamel raises his hand, one finger pointing to the sky, to emphasise the importance of what he is about to say:

"In Sufi vocabulary natural death is called 'death by necessity,' sleep is called the small death, and meditation is called 'voluntary death.' Death, when mentioned in Sufi texts, is not the one that is followed by burial. It refers to the state of trance reached during deep meditation directed by an experienced master, when the body is in a cataleptic state."

Sheikh Kamel refers to the story of the merchant and his bird. He then concludes:

"To accomplish the journey through the infinitely wide supra-sensible kingdoms, the human being must pass through a tunnel that connects the material world to other dimensions. This requires the intervention of death. But death is a departure without return. A simulated death must thus be produced. This simulation consists in the act of bringing the soul to a state of deep hypnotic trance by reducing the heartbeats and the respiratory rhythm to their minimum level.

This self-hypnosis is a specific method that the Sufis learn after long years of practice. Thus they can follow the movement of the soul separated from its skin envelope. But to reach this state, one must follow an unwritten 1000 year old teaching. It is transmitted orally from the master to his disciple. Through gradual learning and exercise of certain practices that have been kept secret, the Sufis reach a point where they can overcome the drives of their primitive instincts and abolish their egocentrism. This is a spiritual purification."

Sheikh Kamel adds:

"To clear up some of the most difficult or abstract aspects of this subject, let me tell you one more very significant story from the Masnavi[21]."

The Chinese And The Roman Artists

One day a king wanted to decorate the grand hall of his new palace. Two groups of artists applied to perform this work. The king decided to give each group one half of the hall. He ordered that a great curtain be placed in the middle of the hall, to make two equal parts. Each part of the hall was assigned to a group.

One group was Chinese, and the other was Roman.

The Chinese, who had great experience in this type of work and were considered specialists in their brilliant empire, and started immediately. They requested much lacquer, paint, gold leaves, and other supplies. They worked day and night, in deep concentration, showing great aptitude of organisation and teamwork.

During this time, Romans had requested no budget, and they could be seen resting casually and roaming around, totally relaxed. This situation spurred the curiosity of the people at the royal court. They were impatiently waiting for the day when the king would come and uncover each work.

On the day the king arrived, he first uncovered the Chinese side. He stood there, overwhelmed by the fine design and lush colours. The work of the Chinese artists was a true masterpiece, a pure wonder!

When he ordered the heavy curtain removed from the Roman side, he was amazed to find that decoration was identical to the Chinese, but more

---

21 Masnavi vol. 1

luminous and with moving reflections that gave the work more life and splendour. The Roman artists had used mirrors, giant mirrors that reflected the marvellous work of the Chinese artists!

Mowlana explains that the Sufis are like the Roman artists: they purify, and polish their hearts until they are clean as mirrors, reflecting the splendours of the divinity. The act of polishing the heart requires the negation of the Sufi's pride and individuality. The mirror is the symbol of this act of negation.

12 - Explanation of the Principle of Negation

Tonight, before beginning, Sheikh Kamel requests that his audience be especially attentive. He wants to philosophise a bit. He says:

"In the story of the parrot that I told you on the second night of the month of Ramadan, Mowlana introduces the main aspects of Sufi seeking methods which are in opposition to the rational methods based on logical argumentation, where reflection is cantered on the movement of the mind from the known toward the unknown.

The rational person deduces C from A and B which he uses as thesis and antithesis to establish the synthesis represented by C. Man moves in a one-way direction, trying to shed light on the dark zones of the world, which are concealed from his knowledge. The starting point of this approach is positive, and the final point is negative.

Mowlana shows another way, where the starting point is negation and the final point is affirmation. For him, dissolution is the key to knowledge. We do not exist for the purpose of experiencing the non-existent; rather, we renounce ourselves, in order to understand existence. We choose insanity to learn the nature of reason. We knock at the door of rapture to reach the summit of wisdom.

'How can the negation and the affirmation of a thing be combined and reconciled with relativity and difference? It is possible to deny and affirm the

same thing: when the point of view is different, the relation is double.' A Quranic verse[22]

'You have not shot the arrow when you, have shot the arrow' is relative: it is a negation and an affirmation; both are right. You have shot it because it was in your hand; you have not shot it because 'Hagh' (=God) has manifested His power.

Your hand is your hand, and shooting is Our intention.

Are the negation and the affirmation of this action both true, because of these two relations?[23]*"*

There Is No Dervish (Sufi) In The World

"*Fanâ*" means "annihilation", or "dissolution." There is no real translation for "*Baghâ,*" a word that means the continuation of existence after dissolution.

The speaker said:

"There is no Sufi in the world.
And if there is any Sufi in the world,
this Sufi is in reality non-existent.
His essence remains intact and under this aspect he exists,

but his attributes have dissolved in the attributes of the Hou (God)."

I. it is like the flame of a candle in the sun: it is part of the Naught, although, according to logical calculation, it exists. Its essence still exists because if you

---

22 Surah 8, v:17

23 Ed. du Rocher, vol. III, p.756-7, Mirkhani, vol. III p.294.

*cover it with cotton, the sparks will burn the material. But then the luminosity is as if non-existent because it does not give light: its light is annihilated by the sunbeams."*24

By definition, the Sufi is one whose identity has been dissolved in the divinity and the absolute. He has practiced the principle of negation and this has prepared him for a state of complete awareness, unknown to ordinary people. God manifests Himself through the Sufi who has no personal identity anymore. He is one with God and has overcome every form of duality that distances him from God. As such, a Sufi cannot exist, because his existence implies that he is one with God. Thus he has lost his own identity, which has dissolved in the divinity. Physically, he is still there, but he is non-existent from the spiritual point of view: he has reached his goal of unity with God. This unification goes through the denial of his own attributes.

The Minstrel and the Turkish Emir

Using Mowlana's the tale of the minstrel and the Turkish emir, Sheikh Kamel, continues to further develops this subject. There are also in this tale some references to the secrets of mystic music:

"Mystic music, or *"sama,"* begins with the note 'LA' [A] of the scale. 'LA' in Arabic means 'no,' or the most absolute negation. The musician takes his audience from 'LA' to 'ella,' which means 'except,' that is, from negation to affirmation. 'La Elah Ella Allah' ('There is no god except God') is, incidentally, the main *zekr* of Sufi and Muslim mystics.

---

24 Mirkhani, vol. III I p.294, compared with Du Rocher, vol. III p.757.

By this basic negation, the relative is denied, and in the affirmation that follows, the absolute replaces it: the relative, like the Sufi in his *fanâ*, is dissolved in the Absolute of divinity.

With this in mind, here is the story of the minstrel and the Turkish emir:

> *'In the presence of a drunken Turkish emir a minstrel began singing the mysteries of Alast under the veil of a melody:*
>
> *'I don't know if you are the moon or an idol; I don't know what You want of me.'*
>
> *'I don't know how I could serve you. If I keep silent or express you in words.'*
>
> *'It is marvellous that you are not separated from me, and yet, where am I and where are you, I don't know.'*
>
> *'I don't know how you attract me. Sometimes you attract me in your bosom, sometimes in blood.'"*
>
> *So the minstrel spoke only to say 'I don't know;' he created a melody with 'I don't know, I don't know.'*
>
> *The refrain 'I don't know, I don't know' became unbearable and our Turk was tired of this repetition. He jumped up and went to fetch a club to strike the minstrel's head.*
>
> *But an officer stopped his hand and said: 'No, it would be bad to kill this minstrel.'*
>
> *The Turk responded: 'This unending repetition has destroyed my nerves! I will strike his head!' Then addressing the minstrel, he said: 'You idiot! If you don't know, don't say foolish things. And if you know, play some adequate melody. Talk about what you know, you imbecile, and don't repeat continually 'I don't know, I don't know.' Suppose I ask you 'where do you*

come from, you hypocrite,' and you answer: 'not from Bukhara, not from Herat, not from Baghdad, not from Mosul, and not from Taraz.'

You will go on for quite some time saying 'not from.., not from...'

It is enough for you to say where you come from and avoid any other distraction. In this case, it is stupid to develop such a subject!

Suppose I ask you, 'what did you eat for lunch?' and you answer with 'no wine, no roast, no quail, no tharid, and no lentils.' Just tell me what you have really eaten and nothing more! Why all this talk?'

'Because,' said the minstrel, 'I have a secret objective. You can't understand the affirmation of God before you deny everything. I have used the negative so that you understand the exaltation of affirmation. I have tuned my instrument on negation. When you die, your death will clarify the mystery for you![25]

There is no doubt that negation (not being) is the opposite of the being (real). I have done this in such a way that using one of the opposites you acquire knowledge of the other opposite.

Oh you, who possess serenity, if you yearn for this unveiled reality, choose death and tear loose the veil. Not a death that sends you to a grave, but a death of transmutation, so that you can enter the light.

When earth turns to gold, its earthly aspect disappears; when sadness turns to joy, the thorn of sadness disappears.

That is why Mostafa (Muhammad) said: "Oh you, seeker of mysteries, if you long to see a living dead, walking on the earth as living men, who is yet dead and whose spirit has gone to heaven, look at the one whose spirit dwells now-in heaven." When he dies, his spirit will not be transferred, because it has been

---

25 Among the diverse notes of music (Do, Re, Mi, Fa, So, La, Si) the Sufi's music starts with the note "La" (meaning "no") for carrying the person listening, to "ella" (meaning "except by")

transferred before his death: this mystery can only be understood through death, not by the use of reason.

It is a transfer, but not like the transfer of ordinary people moving from one place to another. (But to Hou)[26]

What is "Mâ" in the Arabic language? It is the affirmation of negation.

I am no affirmation, I am without essence and annihilated.[27].

I have found individuality in non-individuality; I have thus woven my individuality in non-individuality[28]

Commentary

The assembly is petrified, simply overwhelmed and Sheikh Kamel can read despair on their faces. Apparently, his apprentice-Sufis, with their practical minds, are completely perplexed by his philosophical explanations. He proposes to clarify this through some added comments:

"In this short story Mowlana unveils the secret of 'No, of negation. Negation is the key to the gate of 'Yes, – affirmation. The one who asserts himself as an individual creates a destructive imagination that imposes limits on the absolute existence and makes it relative. He taints the integrity of the absolute. On the other hand, self-denial is the elimination of this unfounded illusion. Denial does not concern the

---

26 Hou means "Him," it is one of the names of God.

27 Fanâ (or negation) is the transformation of "individuality" or "divinity"; it is what we call the "substantial Evolution."

28 Translated from "Book VI," Masnavi Mirkhani (Tehran, 1331, pp. 42-51), compared to the Masnavi translation "In Search of the Absolute" (Paris: Editions du Rocher, 1990, pp.1422-1423).

essence of the being, but its particularities in time and in space (these are quantity, quality, relativity, origin, appearance, essence...).

Going through the denial of partial limits, the relativity of being dissolved which makes place for the integrity of Existence:

> "[29]*Oh my son, know that everything in the universe is like a container filled to the rim with wisdom and beauty. All things are drops of His beauty, which, because of His plenitude, are not kept hidden behind the veil.*"[30]

---

29 Mirkhani, p.230

30 This subject is not only very interesting, but also very complicated. Like the famous quote, "to be, or not to be," this is the question.

13 - Soul Doctors

On this thirteenth night, Sheikh Kamel speaks thus:

"Most of us take care of our bodies: we exercise, watch the food we eat, avoid pollution and look after our environment. Although 100 years is about the maximum lifespan of the body, which we try to keep in perfect health, the slightest symptom sends us to the doctor.

On the other hand, only a few of us take care of our soul, even though we will live for an infinite length of time in this invisible soul!

There are very simple rules for the strengthening of the soul or astral body, or at least to avoid its degradation by inadequate behaviour. The main thing is to know exactly what to do to nourish and maintain the soul, just as we nourish the body with food and exercise.

Those who do not care for their souls during their lifetime on Earth, and that is the great majority, will be totally at loss when they pass behind the veil. When they recognise their past errors, they will think, 'Had I known...' It will then be too late. There, the possibilities of evolution for a disembodied soul (without physical body) are very different from the possibilities on Earth for incarnate humans, as we all are.

For example, we are regularly vaccinated against the flu, because we know that the illness could temporarily weaken our physical body, and we generally trust our doctor to treat us.

On the other hand, to be healed, very few entrust their souls to the mystics – supposing they know a mystic! But this is necessary to avoid long lasting damage from inadequate behaviour and ignorance of what is good and what is bad for the invisible body that we all possess. The soul is our most precious belonging, because it is our vehicle for eternity. How can we move through the sky if our airplane is broken or used up, even before we have a chance to leave the ground? You would then wait indefinitely for a good soul to come and help you. This is not a happy prospect. Yet, it is a reality, for example, when we see those lost to alcohol and drugs, which literally destroy the astral body!

The real mystic, the experienced master, sees the continuity of life beyond death. For him, there is no veil between our world and the post-physical world. He has the authorisation and the mission, granted to him by higher spirits representing the divinity, to tell us what he sees, without expecting compensation in return (otherwise, he is a charlatan!), and to advise us on a personalised path to nourishment of our souls.

This spiritual food is varied: concentration on an image to focus the spirit and establish a connection with the source of spiritual energy; meditation, which helps us to rid ourselves of parasitic thoughts and detach from the things of this world; repetition of a formula, absolutely individual and corresponding to our nature and the needs of the moment called *zekr* by the Sufis, to raise the vibration rate of the soul and to activate its latent possibilities: eventually, periods of fasting, a well-known method, meant not only for the cleansing of body from toxins, but also and essentially to strengthen the astral body; avoiding consumption of alcohol and some meats, like pork, which blur and slow the soul's vibration rhythm and, as a result, prevent the eventual elevation of the soul to higher plains. As such the soul will remain in the lower astral level, on the edge of our material world, where invisible creatures dwell and whose company is certainly undesirable.

Of course, anyone who does not practice any of these exercises will not necessarily suffer immediate consequences. He may go on happily and in good health for a very long time; but this does not reflect on his astral body.

In reality, one looks the same in the invisible world as in the material world.

The sailors of African origin in the Persian Gulf have a proverb:

> *"The one who lives like a pig will die like a pig, and on the other side he will be like a pig, and nothing more."*

Sheikh Kamel is satisfied with this last proverb. He looks right and left into the eyes of the Sufis to evaluate its impact. The sheikh and his assembly all sip their teas, and then he speaks again:

"If you wish, let us return to Mowlana and his tales so full of teaching. Here is the tale of the Arab from the Desert and the Caliph of Baghdad."

The Bedouin And The Caliph Of Baghdad

> *The wife of a Bedouin says to her husband: "We have rain water in the pitcher; it is your most precious property, your capital and your good.*
>
> *Take this pitcher of water and present yourself to the king of kings and give it to him as a present.*
>
> *Tell him, 'this is all we possess. In the desert there is nothing more precious than this water.'*

Although his treasure is full of gold and jewels, he certainly does not have such water; it is rare!"

The husband was full of pride (he thinks) "Who has such a present! It is indeed worthy of a king such as he!"

The woman did not know that there is a big river full of water as sweet as sugar along the public road in the city of Baghdad. It flows like a sea through the city, with plenty of boats and fishing nets.

"Go to the sultan and contemplate his pomp and majesty!"

After having saved his treasure from bandits and preserved it from stones on the road, he came without delay with his pitcher to the domain of the Caliph. When the Bedouin had come from the far desert to the doors of the palace, he said: "Oh you, whose face shows the signs of nobility. Oh you, whose face is more radiant that pure gold of Jafar. Oh you, whose contemplation equals a hundred other visions, it would be right to spend thousands of dinars just to see you once. Oh you, who have become seers by the grace of God, who have come from God to exercise magnificence, to transmute the copper of human beings into gold, by the way of the alchemy of your gaze. I am a stranger, and I have come from the desert hoping to obtain the blessing of the sultan.

The perfume of his blessing has filled deserts; even the sand corns have received a soul.

I have come here to ask for money, yet as soon as I arrived, I was aghast by this vision. I have brought water as a present, hoping for bread, and the hope of bread has led me to the highest place in paradise!"

When the Caliph saw the present and heard the story of the Bedouin, he filled the pitcher with gold and gave him other presents too. He said; "Give him this pitcher filled with gold, and on his way back, make him cross the Tigris."

> *When the Arab stepped on the boat and saw the Tigris, he prostrated, ashamed, and said: "Oh! How marvellous is the goodness of this king, and yet, an even greater marvel is that he has taken that water!"*[31]

Mowlana's Message

In this parable, the pitcher is understood as a symbol of the physical body. The Tigris represents the unlimited knowledge, which is the privilege of the spiritual world and those who have access to it.

If we consider the work of Mowlana Rumi, we notice that the 27,500 verses from his Masnavi have the principal objective of conveying a fundamental message to the reader.

With the five senses of the physical body and aided by intelligence, we can understand questions relative to the sensuous and material world. But our knowledge is limited to that level. There is no way, with only these tools, to approach the supra-sensible world. The Baghdad of the parable, where the Tigris flows, symbolises the unlimited direct knowledge. We must first empty the pitcher of its cloudy water and fill it again with gold. We must first purify the body and empty it of rational, conscious knowledge before pretending to have access to the Tigris and knowledge of the supra-sensible world. Mowlana writes:

> *This pitcher is the symbol of our various sorts of knowledge, and the Caliph represents the Tigris of God's knowledge.*
>
> *We take our filled pitchers to the Tigris! Even if we do not consider ourselves to be donkeys, fix what we all are!*

---

31 Masnavi, translation Ed. du Rocher, vol. 1, p.230.

After all, the Bedouin could be excused, because he was not familiar with the Tigris, the big river.

Had he known of it, the way we do, he would have broken his pitcher against a stone. 32

The more logic we use, the further we move from answers to the supra-sensible world and knowledge of the divinity. To get closer, we must suspend the five senses – empty the pitcher and short-circuit the mind. Thus, a state of trans-awareness will appear: a modified, expanded awareness on a level incompatible with and unapproachable from the state of ordinary consciousness. Let us again listen to Mowlana:

*"What is this pitcher? It is our limited body full of the briny water of our senses; a pitcher with five spouts: the five senses. Keep the water pure to find an open passage to the sea and to become like the sea, in such a way that when you bring your present to the King, he finds it pure and takes it! After this, its water will become without limit, and a hundred worlds will be filled from your pitcher. Cork the spouts and preserve the water in the pitcher from painful reality."*33 *"...We take our filled pitchers to the Tigris! Even if we do not consider ourselves to be donkeys that is what we are!"* 34

---

32 Ibid, p.229

33 Ibid., p.226

34 Ibid., p.230

14 - An Allusion To The Principle Of Negation

Tonight, the Sheikh continues with the subject of last night's discussion. He begins with a quotation from the Masnavi:

If take Arab had only seen a single tributary of the divine Tigris, he would have broken the pitcher. Truly! He has broken it!

Those who have seen it are always out of themselves with awe. And as such, they have thrown a stone at the pitcher of their own existence.

Oh you, who, because of envy, have thrown a stone to the pitcher you see that the pitcher has become more perfect, after having been broken! The pitcher is broken, but water has not spilled out. From this break, one hundred integrities have emerged. Each piece of the pitcher dances in ecstasy, although under the aspect of reason this seems absurd.

In such a state, neither the pitcher nor the water is manifest.

Think about it. And God knows the answer.[35]

The sheikh explains that Mowlana alludes to the fact that when we look for perfection, we must first empty the receiver. Then Mowlana leads us one step further. He explains that what hinders a pitcher's better knowledge of the ocean are the limits imposed by its own capacity.

"It is clear that with a glass already full, one cannot empty the ocean's reserves. But even with an empty glass, a big one, there are still limitations because of the restricted capacity of the glass. This is why we must not only empty the glass, but also break it into a thousand

---

35 Ibid., p.230

pieces! To empty, to deny and to annihilate: this is the beginning of the mystical journey. Nobody can take a step toward the invisible world by leaning on the walking stick of philosophical and rational reasoning.

We are like the Bedouin. Like him, we live in a very limited world. We are often satisfied with it, knowing nothing else. We consider precious some of the material goods we possess. However, these have no value on the other side, in the land of the Caliph who stands for our Lord ruling the kingdom of heaven. That other world hides such a wealth beyond our imagination.

If we sincerely ask for help, we receive much: the Caliph gives generously to those who make the effort to come to him. But the road to him is long and dangerous. It is the way of the *salek*, the walker on the spiritual path. This path, with its mirages and risks of getting lost, after many stops in the desert, leads to the kingdom of heaven.

But once the journey is complete, the Bedouin becomes another man. His vision of the world has widened. He knows of the other world and its wealth; the value of everything he knew before has now become relative. He will go back to the desert to tell his people, who will have problems believing him, what he has experienced."

> *Consider the senses of those for whom God has prepared gardens under which streams flow.*
>
> *Our senses and perceptions as such represent only one drop in these streams.*[36]

---

36 Ibid. I, p 230

Figure 5 – The Tomb of Rumi in Konya, Turkey

15 - The Grammarian And The Navigator

Tonight Sheikh Kamel criticises arrogance and egotism. Once again, he refers to the Masnavi:

Mowlana, he says, wants to point out how important it is to understand that the meaning of this story is not found on the level of intellectual intelligence, because it is of a mystical nature. We must seek practical experience instead of being content with useless verbal discussions. He says:

> *Oh you who dwells is in the desert and who draws briny water, how could you have known the Shatt, the Tigris and the Euphrates?*
>
> *Oh you who has not escaped this fleeting caravanserai, how could you have known about the extinction of the ego, the mystical rapture, and the expansion of the heart?*
>
> *And if you know them, it is because this has been handed down from your grandfather and your father. For you, these names are like the abjad (the alphabet). How simple and evident is the alphabet for all children, and yet its real meaning is far.* [37]

"*This is the story of the grammarian and the navigator,*" says the Sheikh:

The Grammarian and the Navigator

A grammarian stepped onto a boat. This conceited man turned to the navigator and said: "Have you ever studied grammar?"

---

37 Ibid. I, p.230

"No." said he. The other one said: "Then you have wasted all of your life!"

The navigator was very hurt but did not answer at this point.

The wind pushed the boat into a whirlpool. The navigator shouted to thee grammarian: "Tell me, can you swim?" "No," said he. "Oh you, talker, man of fine appearance! Oh you grammarian!" said he "Your whole life is wasted, because the boat is sinking! You should know that what is required here is mahw, (humility) and not nahw (grammar). If you are mahw (dead to yourself), then plunge into the sea, do not fear danger.

Sea water will bring the floating dead to the surface. But what if he is alive? How can he escape the sea?

When you are dead to the attributes of the body, the Sea of divine awareness will raise you to the top.

But, oh you, who has called others donkey, you stand now yourself like a donkey stuck in the mud.

Even if you are the greatest scholar of your era in this world, take heed of the passing world and the passing time.

We have told the story of the grammarian in order to teach you the grammar (nahw) to erase pride (mahw).

In the act of self-dissolution, oh you, respected friend, you will find the jurisprudence of these two sciences.[38]

"The current of life is similar to an ocean. On sunny days, the sea is calm and smooth like oil. At other times, when a storm blows, you could be crushed by a whirlpool. People floating on the surface of the sea may climb into the boat of *welayat* (the way of spirituality) the captain of which is the *wali*, the spiritual guide.

---

38 Masnavi/Mirkhani, vol. 1 p.75 Translation: Ed du Rocherip. 228-9

Because of pure vanity, some people compare themselves the *wali*. They have much knowledge of things, and like our learned grammarian they think that this makes them superior to others. They are furl of themselves and consider themselves to be important. The difference with the *wali* is that he is the only one capable of steering the boat through the storm, avoiding the reefs. Only he can bring the boat to the right port in face of all difficulties.

The *wali* favours and guides those who are humble. He will not help those who are filled with self-importance, those who are so sure to hold the truth and feel superior to others because of their intellectual capacities or their material power, and those that they allow themselves to judge others with arrogance.

When we are humble, the science of the *wali* comes to our aid and guides our existence, making it possible for us to avoid traps, to fare safely on our boat, on both physical and spiritual levels."

> *Mowlana says You must know that each wali is the Noah of his era, and the captain of the boat.*
>
> *You must know that association with people is to risk shipwreck, similar to the Flood.*[39]

"Mowlana means that one who is fully social has a troubled mind; he is much too preoccupied to be able to busy himself with spiritual matters. As Jesus said, 'you must be in the world, but not of the world.' We must live in society, but without getting so involved in it that we forget our real spiritual nature, the existence of our hidden dimension and the necessity of essential evolution.

---

39 Masnavi / Mirkhani / vol. 6 / p. 585

This denial of our social role, which we assume but do not take seriously, is one more aspect of the principle of negation, so important to Mowlana.

This principle is the spine of mysticism. We must suppress pride, eradicate ourselves in the face of God, abnegate in order to assert the unique existence of God and thus dissolve our own identity in our *wali*'s identity. It is by suppressing the duality between the "I" and "He" that there will be nothing except God, like a drop of water dissolving in the ocean. The negation of our limiting individuality opens to us a widened awareness in an infinite universal way."

After a moment of silence, Sheikh Kamel concludes his speech for the night with a concise sentence. This sentence has the mission to remain in the minds of those who listen to him, and inspire them to reflect. He says:

"The implementation of this principle passes concretely through the practice of meditation."

And the symbol of this principle of negation is the mirror.

Figure 6- A Carved Wooden Window in Alhambra, Spain

16 - Man In The Image Of God

This is what Sheikh Kamel says on this sixteenth night of the month of Ramadan:

"The principle of negation is not the purpose of Sufism, as such. It is simply a way to exploit the hidden treasures in ourselves.

According to the Bible, God created man in His own image. And the Qur'an says that man is the vicar of God.

This does not mean that every human being is a vicar of God, but that each person has the latent potential of becoming so. The one who starts the substantial quest and becomes an accomplished human being, shows through his or her deeds and gestures the superior attributes of divine beings.

As long as a man remains a prisoner of his social, familial, ethnic, and cultural engagements, he is alienated, unaware of his self. Negation is the act of challenging this self-ignorance and incomprehension.

Man is a double sided being, with one visible side and one invisible side. Given this, we can compare him to an iceberg: the most important parts are hidden under the surface of the ocean. Because we see only a small part of the iceberg does not mean that the other, more important part, hidden under water, does not exist. That part is simply hidden, inaccessible to the eyes and to the senses of the one who looks on the surface.

The principle of negation is not a question of renouncing beauty, pleasures, and wealth and what it brings us. The Sufis are not specifically ascetics.

In fact, the principle of negation is the act of widening our awareness to hidden and undiscovered aspects of existence: the principle of negation must be understood as a positive postulate.

Man is the seat of unlimited power. It is enough to know how to exploit this power and make it operational. In spite of the metaphor, which is misleading, the Sufis are by no means in search of death or suicide. They are not opposed to social relations and do not live in seclusion in mountain caves far from civilisation. They are simply in search of the essence, and do not rely uniquely on appearance. They are, as Jesus said, 'in the world, but not of the world.' They are citizens like any other; they respect their social and familial engagements. Yet, they take some distance and avoid getting overly involved in the business of the world to avoid interference in their spiritual life caused by exhausting material preoccupations.

As in the story of the Arab of the desert, the practical aspect of the principle of negation is an invitation for us to go to the Tigris and draw from its unlimited knowledge, instead of being satisfied with the briny spring at home in the desert. We must ignore the jar if we want to reach the unending flow of the Euphrates. We must surpass ourselves to discover the endless springs at the core of our being."

The Deception Of Resemblance

"Leaves fall in autumn. Let us imagine that they fall on a pond and cover the surface and all around the banks. A man walking in the woods on a carpet of dead leaves will not notice the limits between the bank and the water; he will fall into the cold water if he has only paid attention to the appearances and trusted his sensory perception. Appearances are misleading and unfortunately our mind is often deceived.

An accomplished person has a normal outer appearance; he eats, sleeps and lives like us. But this does not mean that we are all comparable to those who have substantially developed their essence. Our resemblance stops here, because our logic limits itself to appearances, while the accomplished man is in permanent connection with the spiritual world. He lives in parallel between the two levels of existence and on both levels of experience: the normal physical level and the spiritual level. As soon as he closes his eyes, his awareness embarks on a journey, visits worlds inaccessible to us, seeks advice from superior spirits, transcends space and time, and uses faculties that are the privilege of developed free spirits. He returns to his body with the knowledge of supra-sensible matters that make him much different from the poor parrots that we are, imprisoned in the cage of our physical body. On this subject, Mowlana has many stories, such as the following:

The Oil Merchant's Parrot [40]

An oil merchant had a beautiful multi-coloured parrot that kept watch over the shop when he went on errands for his business. One day, coming back from a journey, he found his shop in chaos. All the oil jars were upside down. He accused the poor parrot, without knowing that in fact a cat had caused this. The faithful bird could do nothing against the cat. Overcome by rage, the oil merchant beat the poor bird until most of its beautiful feathers fell from its back.

---

40 Mirkhani, Vol I

A few days later, a Sufi came into the shop, his head shaved, in line with the rule of his brotherhood. Astonished by this strange appearance, the parrot said: "How come you are bald and featherless like me? Have you been accused of having put the oil jars upside down?"

This question amused all the clients, but it hides an important message:

In effect, the parrot compares himself to the Sufi. By a single detail of physical aspect, he unites the condition of a Sufi to the condition of a parrot, unable to imagine how far apart the existence and the essence of a Sufi are from those of a featherless parrot.

We are often like this parrot. We think: 'This one is like me, he has the same experience of life as I do, because he resembles me, and we have common physical aspects.' Our logic is essentially based on sensory perceptions that consider only the external appearance, without seeing what hides behind it.

To illustrate the principle of the deception of resemblance better, Mowlana takes the lion, 'king of the beasts,' as an example. He makes a radical distinction between the Lion of God and the Lion of the Jungle. The first one fights his impulses and carnal desires, while the second attacks others[41]. After having explained this important distinction, using other parables, he further explains that we become a Lion of God by performing exercises, in solitude and secret, to develop our essence. People who do not recognise this substantial transmutation in the existence of the one who has travelled on the path to perfection consider him as one similar to themselves.

---

41 Masnavi, vol. 1

Figure 7- Fountain de los Leones, Alhambra, Spain.

17 - The Lion In The Desert And The Bowl Of Milk

Tonight, on the seventeenth night of the month of Ramadan, the Sheikh resumes his teaching on the same subject as the preceding night. He tells his audience that he will recount tales of lions.

"The word *shir* in Persian has two different meanings: lion and milk. Similarly, the word *badieh* means both bowl (a recipient) and the desert. If you combine the words *shir* and *badieh*, you will see that, *the lion in the desert* and *the milk in the bowl* are spoken exactly the same way (*shir dar badieh*). Although a lion in the desert will eat a man who passes, the same man will peacefully drink milk out of a bowl. The first one is a deadly situation, while the second is beneficial nourishment; yete they are both spoken the same way.

Here again confusion comes from the similarity of words, from an aspect that hides the essence and real nature of things. You must agree that a lion in the desert has nothing in common with a bowl of milk. And similarly, a spiritual master has little in common with the man on the street, although they look alike."

The Cow That Became A Lion

A poor peasant owned only one cow. Every evening, the good man took his cow back to the cowshed where there was no window or other source of light. He brought in some fodder, caressed the cow, and went home.

One day a lion came into the cowshed. During the time the peasant took to go and fetch fodder, the lion had eaten the poor cow and taken its place in the cowshed. The peasant came in as usual, put the fodder in front of the animal, caressed the lion, thinking it was his cow, and left without having suspected anything, because it was so dark in there! Well, the peasant believed only his senses, which made no distinction between the cow and the lion.

Because the lion did not react, it was normal for the peasant not to distinguish the lion from the cow. The poor man had only his physical senses to discern one from another, and these, due to the circumstances, were insufficient. In these circumstances, the lion did not expose his true nature, but let the poor man believe him to be a cow.

This little story once again, contains many spiritual symbols.

In the darkness, in solitude, in his mystical retreat, the one who has entered as a simple cow changes into a lion. In the course of the spiritual hardships, he acquires mystical faculties that make him similar to a lion. In contrast, the soul of an ordinary man may be symbolised by a cow. The soul of a *wali*, the spiritual master, a Sufi having gone all the way to the end of spiritual, essential evolution, is symbolised by a lion.

This difference is only perceived by those whose inner eye is open and who see with their heart. For the man of the street, the lion remains a cow, because there appears to be no difference between the one who has brought his ascendant journey to an end and an ordinary man. Most of us are in the darkness of ignorance, and we cannot distinguish a lion from a cow, like the parrot that took a Sufi for one of his own. But if you know the lion, you must respect a certain ethic in his presence.

The Lion's Meal

Once upon a time, there was a lion that ruled the entire jungle, according to his status, the king of animals. The other animals discovered what food he

The Lion In The Desert And The Bowl Of Milk

liked and killed a gazelle, which they offered to the King. The wolf spoke first, declaring: "You are the king of animals, it is normal that you receive the best part of the feast then I will take the next best, because I am..." But he did not have time to finish his sentence. As soon as he said, "I am" the lion jumped on him and tore him apart!

Then the fox spoke: "We are nothing, we are useless, the whole of the gazelle is for you!"

"They are intelligent words" the lion said. "As a reward, I give you the part of the game."

The wolf had made a fatal error: he had affirmed his identity in the presence of the lion. In doing so, he had created duality, a distance that made him unworthy of sharing the royal banquet. The fox, on the other hand, began with the negation of any individual, restricting identity. Thus he may sit at his lord's banquet. This is an important, parable on the principle of negation, which is the starting point of the mystic life. The lion is the *wali*, the spiritual master, representing God on Earth. Through mystical retreats, and spiritual hardships, his soul has grown and transmuted as a lion; he has identified himself-with his Lord.

This brief tale provides a key to essential evolution. You must first eliminate individuality, any form of personal pride, before finding the power of identification with your lord, as a drop of water identifies itself with the sea. One drop of water that would assert itself in front of the ocean would, in effect, separate itself from the immensity of the ocean. On the other hand, self-negation and assertion of the exclusive existence of the ocean would affirm the drop's dilution into this ocean; it would then reach awareness of being the whole ocean. Just as the drop becomes the ocean, because it annihilates itself and dissolves into the ocean, we have the capacity to become the universe and to become

God by denying our own individuality in the face of God's immense universe.

This is the theme of Mowlana Balkhi's thought.

18 - Wealth And Poverty

On the eighteenth night, Sheikh Kamel discusses riches:

"What the Sufis actually seek is spiritual wealth. The way to this is through poverty. It must be made clear that the kind of wealth and poverty sought by the Sufis has absolutely no socio-economical connotations. In fact, seen in the context of his existence, every creature is poor. Under this aspect, God (or the Absolute and Necessary Existence), is the Rich Being and creation exists thanks to the continual existential effusion by the Unique Being. But the human being is not conscious, and because ignorance demands existential autonomy. This expectation hinders his substantial growth. Sufism teaches to draw at the inexhaustible sources of divine riches. Thus we must go through poverty in order to become rich.

For those whose supra-sensorial perception is well developed, the universe has no limit. He is free and with all his essence he feels the real meaning of freedom. He flies above the material world and goes higher, in the direction of the sun, irresistibly attracted by light, like a butterfly. But those who have not yet applied the principle of negation to their own lives cannot have this experience; they never take such a journey to where the *Simorgh* dwells. They are content with their daily preoccupations – nothing more."

Figure 8- Simorgh(Thirty Birds)

{This design is known as the Crystal Simorgh and is the award of Fajr Film Festival}

19 - Thirty Birds

The talk on the nineteenth night concerns the well-known mythical bird called the *Simorgh*

Sheikh Kamel begins to speak:

"In his famous text, 'The Language of the Birds', the Persian poet Attar tells the story of a *houpe*, a little orange coloured bird with a tassel of feathers on his head. This bird has a very special place in Sufi symbolism. It is the messenger of Solomon, a bird of good omen, in charge of bringing good news and guiding others on the right way. The *houpe* says Attar, gathered the birds one day and urged them to follow him in the quest of the king of the birds, the famous *Simorgh* who dwells on top of a very high mountain, called Qaf.

The *houpe* told them he knew the way to the high mountain Qaf, and a multitude of birds followed him. But there were many temptations on the way: a field of flowers to collect nectar, a cool and quiet stream to quench their thirst and rest by, tall trees providing shade and protection. At each place, some of the travellers stayed behind, held by the appeal of material things. The number of traveling birds reduced progressively. A great majority of them, too attached to Earthly matters, found various excuses to avoid following the front group, the real truth seekers, those who truly yearning to join their king. When they arrived at the domain, high on the Qaf Mountain, there were only thirty of them left.

These thirty birds found themselves facing a mirror and realised that the *Simorgh* was their own reflection in that mirror. What they had come to find on top of the mountain was in fact themselves, transformed through the journey! This is the definition of the word *Simorgh*, which in Persian means thirty birds. This story is an allegory of the travel of the soul out of the body on the way to essential evolution, until the state of perfection is reached at the end of the way.

Many begin the journey when a guide calls, yet just as many give up soon thereafter or temporarily, or are definitively diverted from their soul on the way to evolution. In the end, the guide brings a limited number of disciples to the mountain of evolution. The way is hard and full of obstacles that discourage most of them. The most motivated will resist: the close circle of disciples that surround the guide - the *houpe* of the parable - like the apostles who followed Jesus on the road of Galilee.

Yet those who travel the way are transformed by the journey. They undergo, without return, an essential evolution. That is characterised by the opening of the faculties of their soul, the vision of ever-higher spiritual worlds, the widening of their field of perception, and the acquisition of a direct way of perception of the visible and invisible worlds that surround them. When, after many years of effort, they like the birds in Attar's parable, that the real goal was their own transformation. They had looked for the divinity outside of themselves, somewhere in the higher spiritual skies, and in the end they see that this divinity is hidden in the depths of their own hearts. The way of essential evolution has made the actualisation of this divinity possible, the divinity with whom they are now one and from whom they have direct knowledge, impossible to translate into words, far beyond what the five physical senses perceive.

At this ultimate level of his spiritual evolution, the mystic see not only God in his own self, but also at his own place, without even seeing himself any longer."

20 - Ali Son Of Abu Taleb

It is the twentieth night of the month of Ramadan, the eve of the anniversary of the death of the most important person in Muslim esoteric thought. Indeed the nineteenth day of the month of Ramadan is a very important date for all Muslims, especially for the Shiites, and for the Sufis.

At dawn on the nineteenth day of the month of Ramadan, in a mosque in Koufeh, a city near Baghdad, in Iraq, Ali, son of Abu Taleb received deadly blow on the head as he was doing his morning prayers. He died two days later. Having answered questions of his disciples, and having designated his son Hassan as his successor, he parted from his physical body. He was the greatest Sufi master of initiation, cousin and son-in-law of the Prophet of Islam and also his spiritual heir.

On this occasion, Sufis stay up the whole night between the eighteenth to the nineteenth of Ramadan, and the whole night between the twentieth to the twenty first: they meditate to connect themselves to the spirituality of their Imam, their Pole, and the one who is considered the Jesus of his time and the vicar of God on earth.

In Sufi exegesis, Ali is a unique personality; no one is his equal. He represents God in all aspects. The human being cannot access God, but he can know His divinity by knowledge of Ali. A sentence attributed Ali (*rewayat*) states: "The one who knows my light will know God."

There is another reason why the Sufis cherish the eighteenth and the twenty-first nights of the month of Ramadan. The first time the Qur'an was revealed to the Prophet was during the month of Ramadan on one of these nights. One of these nights is called the night of measure, because during this night, the beings were created in the imaginal world that dominates the whole universe. According to Quranic verses, the spirits, the souls, and the angels come to our world on that night that, spiritually, is more valuable than thousand months. It is for this reason that Sheikh Kamel orients his discussion on detailed explanations of Sufism. This is what he says:

"Sufis seek God's light everywhere; the shortest way to this the act of opening of the heart. In the eyes of biologists and medical doctors, the heart is only a sort of pump, to be replaced if necessary with little artificial machines. To the Sufis, the heart is the junction point where the energetic body and the elementary body come together at a point situated in the centre of the heart. When the soul descends and enters the body of a baby in his mother's womb during the third month of pregnancy, it seeks refuge somewhere in the heart. The more the child grows physically, the more latent capacities of the soul have the potential to grow.

The Sufi method makes it possible for travellers in the esoteric world to develop these capacities and to let the chid grow in their heart. This is the way the Sufi observes his heart. The one who has an open heart becomes a sun on Earth, because an inexhaustible source of light flows from his heart to his head. He (or she) becomes a man (or woman) of light Because of this inner light, he becomes familiar with the beings of light, such as angels and saints. Through light, he will come to know his master, his imam, his prophet and his Lord."

After a short break, the Sheikh resumes:

"The Sufi method rests on four pillars: *Zekr, Fekr, Moraghebeh*, and *Mohassebeh*. Although every Sufi knows this thousand-year-old method, I will use the followings nights, beginning tomorrow, to open the door of comprehension of these practices a bit more."

21 - Zekr

The following night, the Sheikh speaks as planned:

"*Zekr* means "remembrance," as opposed to "forgetting." This word appears often in the Qur'an. It has many other meanings, but for the Sufis it is the act of concentrating on the divine name inscribed in the heart. Each name has its own particularities and specificities. Only the master knows the secret of these words, and only he knows what to teach each disciple.

Remembering God, by concentrating on his name, brings an unintentional forgetting of the world. In opposition to this, one who remembers a simple thing, and focuses his attention on anything, necessarily forgets God. He will only remember God when his material problems cause him difficulties. He then remembers God for the purpose of asking for help. This has nothing to do with *zekr*. The Qur'an teaches us something else: it says '*Remember your Lord when you forget (the rest)*'[42], and it also says '*turn to no one else when you invoke Allah.*'

A Sufi always remembers God because of the love he has for Him in his heart. The more he meditates on his heart, the more room he creates for love. After some time, his heart becomes entirely filled with divine love and contains nothing but this love. About this, Hafez says:

> '*The grief of your love is found only in a happy heart; in search of this grief we seek a happy heart.*'

---

42 Surah 18, v:24

In other words, we cannot have the heart oriented towards opposing directions, in the direction of unity and direction of plurality. Plurality concerns the business of this world the management of which is a question of rationality. With unity, it is a question of concentration of the spirit on a single word, a single image, and a single subject: God. It is said that Sufis lead a bi-dimensional life; this is true, because they assume the responsibility for their marital and social life, while simultaneously their hearts beat absolutely and totally for the love of God."

The Sheikh adds:

"There are four categories of *zekr*: spoken *zekr*, *zekr* practiced in the heart; *zekr* practiced in solitude; and *zekr* practiced in a group setting.

"There are three categories of silent *zekr*: *zekr anfossi*, practiced through the regulation of respiration; *zekr galbi*, practiced through control of the faculty of imagination; and *zekr hamayeli* brings the whole body into action. The common point between these three types of silent *zekr* is the concentration of attention on the heart.

The vocal *zekr* is based on bodily practice: the repetition, a defined number of times, of a word or sentence. This type of *zekr* follows a specific rhythm. Some Sufi orders use musical instruments to accompany the *zekr*. But our order uses neither music nor vocal *zekr* practiced in group."

The Sheikh says:

"The Qur'an invites believers to practice their daily prayers very seriously, because this practice orients the person to purity and away from barbarous acts. Once people get used to goodness and benevolence, the Qur'an makes them move towards *zekr*, which is way to develop the latent faculties of their souls. Thus, *zekr*, is more important than *salat* (prayer), just as university is more important than high school. Here is a Quranic verse: '*Prayer keeps human beings away from abject and shameful actions, whereas Allah's zekr is absolutely the greatest*'[43].

After this reminder, there is a verse inviting believers to practice *zekr* continuously. They learn how to practice the *zekr* of the heart, which repeats itself automatically day and night, in sleep or awake. The Qur'an says: '*After prayer, practice Allah's zekr whether you are standing, seated, or lying down*'[44].

In other verses, believers are invited to practice their *zekr* at times of deep meditation: at dawn and late in the afternoon: '*Invoke often your Lord, and go deep into remembering at dusk and at dawn*'[45]. And: '*Practice the zekr of your Lord at dawn and late in the afternoon*'[46].

There are other verses of the Qur'an that mention esoteric meditation. We will return to them later."

The Influence Of Zekr

Sheikh Kamel resumes:

"The soul in the heart is like a seed placed in a clay pot that later becomes a plant and grows naturally. But like any other plant, it might be attacked by parasites. It must be permanently watched and guarded

---

43 Surah 29, v:45

44 Surah 4, v:103

45 Surah 3, v:41

46 Surah 76, v:25

by clever hands. The *zekr* is like a well-treated and healthy plant that gardeners graft on the stem of another plant. Through this action, the original plant stops growing while the grafted plant grows on the stem of the first one.

Let us make another comparison. The *zekr* is like an elixir alchemists use to transmute copper into gold. The master who gives a *zekr* is similar to a gardener or an alchemist.

But this esoteric alchemy works only through a *zekr* placed in the heart, not through a verbal *zekr*."

The Sheikh presents another example:

"The Japanese catch oysters, open the shell, and put a sand corn in it. Then they return the shell to the sea. Two years later, they bring it back to the surface. There, in solitude and void, the small, formerly insignificant corn is transformed into a priceless pearl.

Alchemy is nothing more than the transmutation of an ordinary object into something valuable. The human soul is transmutable and this happens through an essential evolution, such as the one offered to us by the Sufi method."

The Sheikh stops, takes a sip of his hot tea, and continues his explanation. In his Sufi order called *Nematollahi*, the Sheikhs generally teach their disciples a vocal *zekr*. Still, these *zekrs* must be practiced in silence and not spoken out loud. In practicing this *zekr*, the disciple must repeat the *zekr* a precise number of times, as indicated by the sheikh.

But besides this compulsory practice, the Sheikh authorises the disciple to practice the *zekr* tirelessly if he wishes. This practice is meant for mental and intellectual preparation of the disciple for esoteric understanding of the word's meaning.

In a second teaching phase, the Sheikh teaches the *zekr* of the heart to the disciple who has shown his will and his serious interest. This teaching requires that the disciple be initiated into the order.

The Sheikh continues:

> *"The silent zekr has two phases. The first one integrates the breathing rhythm. It is called anfossi – respiratory. The disciple must become aware that each one of his breaths is necessarily accompanied by his zekr. The divine names and the sentences used in this type of zekr have a specific particularity that makes them to be adapted to the respiration; in rhythm with every inspiration and each expiration of his breathing.*
>
> *"In the morning and in the evening, humbly and silently in your soul, perform the zekr of your Lord without raising your voice, and do not be one of the careless"*[47].

This method of controlled breathing calms the heart and neutralizes stress. This is the best way to regain self-confidence and to eliminate fear and doubts. It brings unequalled tranquillity to the mind. On this, the Qur'an says: *Believers have hearts that can be comforted with Allah's zekr. Learn that hearts find solace in Allah's zekr*[48].

The second type of silent *zekr* that is taught by the Sheikhs to their more advanced disciples is the one practiced in the heart. This type of *zekr* is more complicated, because it requires the simultaneous

---

47 Surah 7, v:205

48 Surah 13, v:28

concentration on a mental image together with the produced resonance that slowly takes possession of the heart. This type of *zekr* needs at least twelve years to become fruitful, if it has been practiced correctly and regularly according to a precise discipline.

The last type of *zekr*, taught by the sheikh to the most advanced disciples, is a *zekr* composed of two contradictory parts: a *zekr* composed of negation and affirmation. This *zekr* has its principal point situated in the heart; it applies to the whole body, and produces the circulation of inner energies in the channels that lead to the heart. This type of *zekr* is usually practiced in a place of solitude, in retreat and meditation, in a prolonged sitting that may last between 40 and 120 days. In the Nematollahi order, this type of *zekr* is seldom taught and then only at the highest level of essential evolution, because it is very demanding and not every bodily frame can take it. This type of *zekr* injures the body and does not bring much to the soul if the soul has not been prepared beforehand through the *zekrs* mentioned above."

Sheikh Kamel stops suddenly, as if he had revealed secrets. "I have spoken too much," he says, "Although I still have not said much for those who are capable of hearing, this will be enough."

22 - Fekr

On the twenty-second night, the Sheikh describes *fekr*: "*Fekr* means reflection. In Sufi vocabulary, it is a synonym for mental images. Anyone getting initiated into an order learns a *zekr* and *fekr* from his Sheikh. The *fekr* is a support for reflection and meditation. It can also be a mental image for the heart. Thus, in a place designated in his heart by his master, the seeker mentally imprints a name, an image, a face or a personage and a *zekr*. He must begin his esoteric work by focusing on his *fekr* and tirelessly repeating it.

Human beings are requested in the Qur'an to turn their thoughts to the universe and its components: to the stars, to animals, and to themselves, in order to glimpse reality. This reality that is hidden under the veil of each subatomic particles, demonstrates that there is no division in our existence. God is the soul of the whole universe, the All.

Through regular practice, love develops in the heart. With the emergence of love, the *fekr* will materialise. This love is a kind of devotion felt by the disciple in his mind for his master. The image that he was trying to actualise in his heart has automatically come to realise that the seeker cannot set himself free, even for a second, from the thought of his master. Thus his master becomes a bridge between him and the divinity. Any emanation coming from the divine world goes through the master, before reaching the disciple. This Sufi reflection is not intellectual, but imaginative. Esoteric love is reached through the control and mastering of the faculty of imagination. With a *fekr*, the Sufi progressively enters the kingdom of conscious dreams. The mental images used by the Sufis are efficient remedy to mental problems. They bring peace of mind, something that is nowadays much in demand."

Majnoon And The Doctor

Wishing to clarify his message on the subject of Sufi reflection, and on the spiritual relationship established between master and disciple, Sheikh Kamel tells the story of Majnoon, a character known from tales on mystic love.

"Majnoon means crazy, which is the nickname of a man called Ghayss. He has this surname because he fell in love with a young Arab tribe girl named Leyla more than 1000 years ago. The respective tribes of Majnoon and Leyla were arch-rivals. Everyone knew of their love for one another, but they were forbidden to marry or live together, or even to see one another.

The love Majnoon had for Leyla was very deep and strong. He lived permanently, day and night, with the thought of his beloved. He was chased away from his tribe because of this forbidden love. He spent his days in the desert along with the wild beasts, which came to him without any sign of aggressiveness."

The Unity Of The Lover And The Beloved

One day, the Caliph ordered his people to bring Leyla to him; he wanted to judge her beauty himself. As he saw her, he was shocked; he found her very ordinary.

He said to her: 'But you are not so pretty. There are in my harem 1000 young girls much prettier than you. I do not understand how Majnoon could fall in love with you the way he did.'

And Leyla answered: 'You do not understand Majnoon, because you are not him. You must see Leyla through the eyes of Majnoon.'

One day, the family of Majnoon decided to find a remedy to his state and called a doctor. After having visited the patient, the doctor instructed them to have some blood taken, in order to lower the blood pressure and diminish the resulting fever. When the master of this art came to visit him and started his work, he found Majnoon very worried, and asked him the reason for his state of mind. Majnoon answered: '"You know very well that I don't fear being cut by a sword, a sabre, a knife, or anything else, but I fear that if you cut my veins, you involuntarily cut Leyla. You must know that Leyla flows in me, that I am her and she is me. We are one soul in two bodies.'

This story shows to what extend mental images are efficient to root and actualise a thought of somebody or something in the soul of the one who meditates.

The Sufis meditate on the image of a word and, through this act; they go back to the source, to the master who represents, as personification and materialization, the finality of their quest. On this subject, Mowlana tells his disciple Hessameddin Chalabi:

> *"Oh you, light of God and sword of the way, take one sheet of paper to describe the Pir (the master). Write about the master who knows the way. Choose your master and consider him as the way itself."*[49]

In this text, Mowlana signifies that the way, on which the disciple starts, has already been taken by the Sheikh, who is himself a personification of the way that the disciple carries in himself. During

---

49 Mirkhani / vol.2

this mystical journey, the disciple permanently centres his mind on his master, thus he will end up finding the master in himself, he will become one with him, and he will reach inner knowledge of him.

This, in Sufi language, is called the unity of the lover and the beloved."

To illustrate this mystical transmutation, Sheikh Kamel tells story from the Masnavi:

> *Once a man knocked on the door of a friend.*
>
> *He asked: "who is knocking?"*
>
> *He said: "It is I."*
>
> *The friend said: "Go away, this is no time to come in here..."*
>
> *He went away and spent one year traveling, far from his friend. He was burned by the flames of separation.*
>
> *Burned and consumed, he came once again to the house of his friend. He knocked at the door full of respect and awe.*
>
> *His friend said: "Who is at the door?"*
>
> *He answered: "It is yourself standing at the door, oh you, thief of hearts!"*
>
> *His friend said: "Now that you are I, come in, because there is not enough room here for two I's."*[50]

The Sheikh stops, looks at his watch and concludes: "Tomorrow will give you some details on *Moraghebeh*."

---

50 Masnavi /.Mirkhani / vol. 1

Figure 9- A Mehrab shaped window, Alhambra, Spain

23 - Moraghebeh (Meditation)

The Sheikh begins his teaching at the same time as the previous nights. He explains meditation:

"Moraghebeh means being attentive and vigilant. In Sufi language, Moraghebeh *means deep and prolonged meditation in a silent and dark place, where no external happening will disturb the concentration. In the Qur'an it is said,* 'God is the Wali of all believers. He leads them from darkness to Light.' *And in another verse:* 'Allah is the light of heaven and earth. He leads with his light the one He chooses.'

Thus, to open the inner eye to Allah's light, we must absolutely keep away from natural light, and sit in the solitude of a dark and silent place. This method is very efficient to awake the child of the heart, if the person sits in meditation for a period up to forty days.

Quarantine

Great Sufi masters, such as Sheikh Najmedin Kobra Ayyubi of Khawrazm, well known under the nickname Sheikh Wali-tarâsh, believe that the most efficient and necessary condition to activate the man or woman of light in the body of a Sufi is meditation in a dark place.

The Sufi who obtains the permission of his master to meditate must try to do by keeping his eyes open all the time, unless he loses control over the muscles. Keeping the eyes wide open over a long time in total darkness, produces specific effects on the components of the retina, on the optic nerve and on the parts of the brain concerned with vision.

Buddhist monks in Zen temples sometimes used to cut their eyelids to be sure to keep their eyes open.

Sheikh Kamal continues:

"I cannot give you any more explanations on the subject. At any rate, nobody can begin such a period of meditation without the authorisation of his master and without being very closely watched by him. It is a general rule concerning all mystics. It was even so for the great prophets of the ancient times, like Moses. Moses was invited to leave his people for a month and reside in the caves of Mount Sinai for an exercise of prolonged meditation. After the thirtieth night, he was ordered to continue his exercises ten more days; thus he achieved a period of quarantine. At the end of this period, he felt ready to face the fight of his Lord. He turned to his invisible master and requested for him to show his face. He received an answer: 'Although you have become capable of seeing the invisible, my light cannot be perceived, even with the supra-sensible organs of your astral body. But as an example, you can contemplate the result of my epiphany on this mountain. If the mountain remains standing when my light is manifested, it will be possible for you to see it.' And when God manifested Himself, the mountain exploded in thousands of pieces and Moses fell to the ground, unconscious.

This story is in detail in the Qur'an and shows us that meditation and quarantine are similar to the technique of the caterpillar that cuts itself from the outside world in the solitude of its cocoon. After a certain time, the alchemy of solitude in dark and silence produces its effects and this creature of the underground, always afraid of the light that always hides in the depth of the earth transmutes into a butterfly with two multicolour wings and a powerful, instinctive longing to fly towards light. All prophets practiced such periods of prolonged meditation. The prophet of Islam, in particular, spent five years, between his thirty-fifth and fortieth year, in a solitary retreat in the Hera Mountains. Zoroaster, a prophet of ancient Persia, received the Revelation as he was meditating on the mountain of Hara. The great Sufi masters who followed the footsteps of the prophets, have also done the same, each one in his time.

For example, Shah Nematollahi Wali spent a significant part of his life in retreat in the mountains of Coobanan, in the region of Kerman, in Iran. And Sheikh Alaodoleh of Semnan went through some 130 periods of quarantine. Sometimes, it might be necessary to spend up to 120 days in prolonged meditation. The act of not talking, eating and sleeping very little, having no exchange with anybody, to be constantly under the supervision of the master and to tirelessly practice a *zekr* composed of negations and affirmations, totally develops the latent faculties of the soul and opens the door to supra-sensorial awareness."

Mohassebeh – Self-Evaluation Of Our Actions

After a short break, the Sheikh resumes, concluding his talk for the night: "What completes meditation is the evaluation, every night after prayers, of our actions of the day. This is called *mohassebeh*. When he continually performs this self-evaluation, the Sufi is always aware of his own evolution. He is his own most severe critic. In opposition to people who criticise others and question their values, the Sufis strive to be better judges of themselves.

With the tools we have learned: *moraghebeh, mohassebeh, zekr,* and *fekr*- Sufis move towards spiritual progress. Because of these characteristics, the Sufi school is based on the principle of essential evolution.

24 - Hozeh

School is at the centre of discussion on this twenty-fourth night: Since the beginning of Islam, there exists in the Middle East an institution that has spanned the centuries: the religious school, called *Hozeh*, which literally means 'the middle.' This tradition even predates Islam, as one finds a similar structure during the time of Mazdien and Sassanid Iran; the schools were led by Zoroastrian priests. The Sheikh elaborates:

"The traditional religious school is centred on a mosque, accessed via a large courtyard in the centre of which is a basin the faithful use to perform their ritual ablutions. Around this courtyard one finds buildings with several small doors, which access modest cells that serve as the students' dormitories. The school is overseen by a respected ayatollah, under whom are other, less important ayatollahs who constitute a professional body, teaching the students various materials such as history geography, literature, and of course theology. In general the students are from various poor families that cannot finance their children's education: these schools are free and the students are housed and fed, even if these amenities are simple and frugal.

In Muslim countries there is a tradition that ten percent of each citizen's earnings belongs to God. This money goes to the religious authorities, and it is by such means that these authorities build economic empires. It is this money that, issued from the generosity of the faithful that supports Quranic schools and modest amenities for the population. For centuries there were, in reality, two kinds of schools, organised according to the same model: religious schools and mystic schools.

The mystic school was run by a spiritual master or by a spiritual master or *pir*, which literality translates as pole. This master was surrounded by 'Sheikhs', holders of spiritual power and working by delegation by the master. In these schools, the students reside in the cells surrounding the central courtyard and are instructed in classical materials, a mystic teaching, and a personalised spiritual regimen. They were the disciples of the master, who taught them how to control their animal nature (*nafs*) and develop their latent faculties. Practicing *zekr* (mental repetition) and *fekr* (visualisation) and isolated, they learned to extinguish their five physical senses to allow expression of the sense of their soul. Some among them eventually obtained the ultimate state of unification with God and the universe.

Throughout the vicissitudes of history, these mystical schools were successively closed in each country in which they flourished. Today, fraternities in which the faithful practice rites in traditional assemblies, preoccupied with defending the *pir* as superior to neighbouring fraternities and claim that their truth is 'The Truth' still exist. With the passage of time and persecutions, pure mysticism has deviated towards a tradition tainted by religiosity and sectarianism.

In addition, the need for true spirituality exists today more than ever, but the numerous aspirants do not know where to find those capable of teaching them the true science of mysteries and to guide them on the spiritual path, as in the time when mystic schools were well off and respected. And besides, God knows the need is great in our times!" Sighs the Sheikh.

Figure 10 - The Tomb of Shah Nematollah, Mahan, Iran

25 - The Closing Of Schools Of Mysticism

On this twenty-fifth night, Sheikh Kamel decides to talk about schools of mysticism in Iran.

"As the Safavids came to reign over Iran, the British Empire had a tremendous influence in this region of the world. The Safavids were the perfect partner of the British against the Ottoman Empire. In contrast to the Turkish Ottomans, who were Sunni Muslims, the vast majority of Iranians were Shiite Muslims. They believed in the *welayat* of Ali, son-in-law of the Prophet. According to them, Ali was the Prophet's spiritual heir and temporal representative of God on earth.

In those days, Iran had no state religion; each city followed its own variety of Islam, as taught by a local sect or brotherhood. The Safavids were duodecimal Shiites. This is based on the occultation of the twelfth Imam, descendent and continuator of the Prophet, who is supposed to return one day as the messiah. Shiite theology does not allow its believers to be involved in politics. The argument is that temporal power must be granted by spiritual power: a privilege of the Imam. Thus, as long as the major occultation of the twelfth Imam is incomplete, no state or person may claim legitimate spirituality. The Shi'a are invited to remain obedient to the existing central power, whatever its nature. Any sort of power, be it democratic or dictatorial, is considered as a usurping the place of the Imam! The Safavids changed this theology, by stipulating that the Shiites had to create their own central power, rather than be ruled by infidels. Under the pretext of defending the Shiite values, they confronted various Sunni nations, at first with the Ottoman Empire. This was in the interest of

Europeans, especially the British. They had used their influence to help install and expand Shiite clergy in the Safavid Empire.

The majority of the people, humiliated by the clergy and their special sort of Shi'ism, starting to hate the Safavids to such an extent that by end of their reign they lost their empire to an army of 3000 poorly armed Afghans.

Following this, a period of instability began, which ended only as the Qadjars, with the help of the British, took power in Iran. They brought with them a new version of Shi'ism from Iraq, called Ussoli. This new version of theology gave much importance to reason, in spite of Quranic verses. Until then, the main role of theologians was to explain and comment on the words of saints: the Prophet, his daughter and the twelve Imams. They thought that 1000 years after major occultation, the twelfth Imam would manifest himself again and put an end to the waiting time. This actually corresponded to the arrival of the Qadjars on Iran.

The coming to power of the Ussoli School brought hope of this manifestation to an end. When the new version of the state theology appeared, many religious schools were created in various cities around the country; the most important of them was called Feizheih, in the city of Qom. The Sufis had been driven out of the country during the Safavid period. Dogmatic religious people were taking over the religious power and almost all brotherhoods left Iran.

During the Qadjar era, the Sufis began to return to Iran, but the religious authorities prevented the King from granting permission for the construction of Sufi *Khanaghahs* (monasteries) and schools of mysticism. The Sufi masters began travelling through the country, going from one city to another, inviting people to practice mysticism.

Many died on the way, but thanks to their tireless efforts, Sufism once again spread in Iran, although without the support of a network of schools.

The creation of Sufi schools is necessary to systematic teaching, because, as the example of Turkey shows, it is very difficult to move directly from a traditional religious society to a modem society.

Mysticism makes it possible to cross this important stage by giving people a greater spiritual opening, unlimited by the yoke of dogmas.

26 - The Truth About Jihad

Tonight Sheikh Kamel has a serious and solemn air. He considers his message on this twenty-sixth night of the month of Ramadan especially important.

"The word *jihad*," he begins, "is nowadays used wrongly, often with a very negative, even terrifying, connotation: as the basis of 'Islamic' terrorism and suicide attacks. The time has come to give the precise spiritual definition of the word *jihad*.

Before embarking on this subject, we must take seriously the dangers caused by arbitrary commentaries of sacred texts. Anyone can read the Qur'an, the Bible, and the Torah, but not anyone can interpret them, because each person projects his own state of mind into his interpretation. People who are ignorant are ruled by the impulses of their ego; they live in the era of ignorance, even if we are in the twenty-first century. Their interpretations of the sacred texts correspond to the low, materialistic level of their comprehension and imagination. You cannot blame the book if the interpretation is false.

Jihad means supreme effort. The root of the word is *jahd*, which means effort. The one who makes considerable effort to reach an important goal is a *mojahid*. The word *jihad* and all derivatives belong to Quranic vocabulary and occur forty-one times in the holy text. *Jihad* is one of the eight pillars of Islam, according to the Shiites. These eight pillars are: *salat* (daily prayer), *soun* (fasting), *khoms* and *zakat* (two religious taxes), *haj* (pilgrimage to the Mecca), *jihad* (all efforts are for God), *amr bil ma'rouf* (the mind is instructed in doing good) *nahi menal monkar* (the ego is prevented from acting badly).

According to the Sunnis, there are five religious obligations: *salat, zakat, soun, haj,* and *jihad.*

The Qur'an describes the believers as people who regularly pray, pay their religious taxes, and make sincere efforts to forego material goods, and suppress their egos on the way to God. In other words, to be a good Muslim, you must respect the importance of *jihad.* But contrary to popular belief, the religious obligation of jihad is outside of any connotation of war. The words designating war in the Qur'an are *harb* and *ketal,* with their derivatives:

> **a) Harb** is a war declared by one person or a group against moral or physical enemies. For example, in in the second surah (set of verses) of the Quran, the 275th verse, *bakara*, strictly condemns usury:
>
> God allowed selling, but not usury[51]. O you believers! Respect the will of God and renounce – if you are true believers- what remains, as profit from usury. But if you do not renounce, be prepared for the war (harb) that God and his prophet consider against you[52].

In another verse:

> *Every time the enemies -try to provoke the fire of war (harb), God puts it out*[53].
>
> **b) Ketal** means to 'engage in war' Ketal can be negative if it aims at scorning justice oppressing the liberty of people. It has

---

51 Surah 2, v: 275

52 Surah 2, 278-9

53 Surah 5, v:64

a positive connotation when it is meant to legitimise defence of life, dignity, goods and another's houses against an invading aggressive enemy. God has allowed Muslims to make war in case of 'legitimate defence.' This happened when the prophet and his companions had to leave Mecca for no justified reason, and in fear of their lives. They were attacked many times by their enemies. The 39th verse of surah *'Haj'* reports this historical event, using the word *ketal* and **not** *jihad."*

Authorisation was given to those who resist militarily (yokateloun) since they have been oppressed and God can grant them victory. [54]

David And Goliath

In various verses the Qur'an refers to the military confrontation between the companions of prophets, in a defensive position, and their invading adversaries with the word *ketal*. One example is the story of the confrontation between, the Israelites, under the leadership of David, and their enemies, headed by Goliath[55]:

Have you not seen the Ancients among the people of Israel after Moses? They told the prophet, "Give us a king, we will fight (Katala) in the way of God." It is impossible for us not to fight (katala) in the way of God, because we have been chased from our houses and separated from our families." Their prophet answered: "God has sent you Saul as king." They said: "We are not capable today of resisting Goliath and his army." But those among them who believed in meeting God answered: "How many times has a small group of men won over a large army with the

---

54 Surah 22, v:39

55 Surah 2, v:245-251

permission of God. God is on the side of those who are patient." With the permission of God, their enemy had to flee and David killed Goliath. God gave David the kingdom and wisdom; he taught him what he wanted.

Just after these verses, the Qur'an makes the following deduction:

If God did not push back certain people using other people, the earth would be filled with corruption[56]. And it is added:

Fight (katelou) on the way to God and learn that God learn that hears and knows everything[57].

Following to the logic of the Qur'an, we may deduce that resistance against injustice, invasion and barbarity is legitimate. Still, it must be emphasised that in these verses the word *jihad* is not used; rather, *ketal* or *mokateleh* are used; in other words, *jihad* does not correspond at all with a military action, neither offensive nor defensive.

The word *jihad* means a very important effort and corresponds to an inner, individual action that each believer is invited to undertake to come gradually closer to the final goal of esoteric ascension towards Allah. On this subject, the Qur'an states:

Those who use their efforts on us (jahadou), we will guide them on our ways[58].

And in the same *surah*, this verse completes the explanation:

The one who does jihad does it for his own good or the one who fights, fights to train his nafs. (Man jahada faennama youiahid le nafseh)[59].

---

56 Surah 2, v:251

57 Surah 2, v:244

58 Surah 29, v: 69

Thus, *jihad* is a war that each believer declares upon his inner-self against his most primitive impulses and instinctive pressures. During this fierce and pitiless fight, the believer tries to develop in himself ever more human and chivalrous attributes, such as friendship, love, generosity, while repressing negative characteristics such as jealousy, hard feelings, and meanness."

---

59 Surah 29, v: 6

27 - Nafs

On this twenty-seventh night, Sheikh Kamel decides to talk more about *jihad*. He says:

"The goal of *jihad* is to fight the *nafs*. In fact, *nafs* does not truly mean "soul," but "ego." It is a part of us that carries instinctive impulses causing barbarity, obscurantism and ignorance. *Nafs* is the most primitive aspect of the human race, corresponding to the reptilian part of the brain. It is under the pressure of the *nafs* that humanity remains, in general, in the domain of the law of the jungle. *Nafs* is in complete contradiction with everything concerning the divine spirit.

Attar, a mystical Persian poet of the 6th century of the Hegira, compares the *nafs* and its characteristics to a jungle dominated by various animals such as the wild wolf, the cunning fox, the bear of sexuality the tiger of aggressiveness, the snake, the bat, the scorpion, etc. The believer's duty is to fight all these animals in himself to turn the jungle of his personality into a garden of flowers and fragrance. Mowlana of Balkh compares the *nafs* to a dragon with seven hundred heads, all of them set against the sky. God has sent the prophets to awaken us from the sleep of egotism and to distinguish the source of danger hidden in our inner-selves. The Qur'an states:

I do not acquit my nafs, because my nafs orders me permanently unhealthy actions[60]. Also, Moses gives this explicit message to the believers: *O you people, come back to your Lord and kill your nafs*[61].

---

60 Surah 12, v:53

To fight against 'the *nafs*, commander of bad actions,' (*ammara bissou*) is a necessary condition for the evolution of the soul towards the superior values of humanity, unity and divinity. By suppressing this first obstacle, the person can progressively become himself, conforming to the image of God; and at the end of a long and difficult journey, he can become God's vicar. That is why the believer will never be able to part with his sword of piety and never renounce this inner fight. The mystics explain that, with the help of *jihad*, the human being can overcome these successive steps to realise and, actualise, in the end, the image of God in himself; it is the only guarantee the traveller has against the vicissitudes of his *nafs*.

The first appeal of the prophets to their disciples is *jihad*, because this supreme effort opens the door to perfection. Thus a *jihad* against our own ego, because our most powerful enemy is our own *nafs*, and as long as we do not manage to control our *nafs*, we will not be able to develop our latent capacities."

The Distinction Between Jihads

In the Muslim tradition, the *sunna* (Muslim tradition), the *foghaha*, or doctors of Islamic law, have distinguished three kinds of *jihad*: the great *jihad* (*jihad al-akbar*), *jihad* against the inner-enemy, (*jihad al-asgar*), the lesser *jihad*, *jihad* against an external enemy to defend the religion, and the noblest of all, the *jihad al-afdal*, which means 'saying the truth in the face of an oppressor'[62].

---

61 Surah 2, v:54

62 Hadith quoted by Muslim and Bokhari

One event of the first wars of Islam shows the importance of the evolving and spiritual meaning of *jihad*. One day there was a confrontation between the Prophet and his companions, with the army of a pagan tribe. The Muslims won the battel. After the enemy's retreat, the prophet found the Muslims very satisfied with their own efforts and their victory. He said to them: '*We go back now from this little battle to the great battle and engage now in the greatest jihad (Farajena menal jihad alasgar ela aljihad alakbar)*'[63]

The Muslims, shocked by these words, answered: '*But this was the worst enemy that we have ever defeated.*' And, Muhammad answered: '*No. your greatest enemy lives in each of you; each one must fight against his own ego (a 'da adovokom alnafs allati baina djanbeikom).*' On this subject, Mowlana of Balkh makes this remark: [64]

> *Consider as little valiant a lion who rushes in the row of enemies. Consider as a real lion the one who overcomes, himself.*

---

[63] Hadith quoted by bayhagi and also quoted by Mowlana in the Masnavi volume I.
[64] Masnawi/vol. 1/ p.38

28 - The Story Of The Two Headed Creature

Sheikh Kamel used the few other remaining nights of the month of Ramadan for a presentation of humanity seen under another aspect. This summary that will also serve as the conclusion of this book.

"The animal brain governs the functioning of the body's various parts.

This cerebral system is called the paleocortex. It is composed of many millions of neurons, linked to one another through intercellular connections. The nerve cells exchange neuronal messages in order to add or diminish, according to the received stimuli, the activity of the various brain centres. These centres are in fact endocrine glands, such as the epiphyses, the hypophyses, the thalamus, the hypothalamus, the cerebellum, the brain stem, and the spinal cord. The highest commanding centre for this meticulous organisation is to be found in the heart of the paleocortex in a small gland called the hypothalamus, which governs the entire existence of the animal.

The five senses are responsible for bringing in the general information from the outer world. There are other nerve networks that bring information concerning the body through the brain stem.

The paleocortex watches over the animal organism and the world around it.

According to instructions given by the brain, the cerebellum commands sympathetic nerves to bring the body in a favourable position, and particularly to bring the executive organs into functioning, in order to trigger the necessary reaction against external provocations.

Thus, the cerebellum acts as an executive officer to the hypothalamus.

The brain's glands regulate the animal's biological clock: sleeping time, waking time, thirst, hunger, and sexual urges (to look for a partner, to copulate, to give birth to children, to feed and teach them how to function). These are some of the functions of the paleocortex.

The organisation of the animal brain acts and reacts under the influence of two primitive instincts: sexuality and aggression, both warrants of individual and species survival.

While sexual behaviour appears automatically and instinctively as soon as the sex glands are developed. On the other hand, the survival instinct appears at birth.

In the jungle, all living beings are permanently on guard to avoid potential danger. Even a light breeze will disturb their sleep and trigger their aggression. When an animal moves to a destructive action, it exploits the totality of its body, via its aggressiveness. The animal's whole body is an executive machine, commanded by, the paleocortex. The tail, the teeth, the beak, the claws, the nails are natural means that serve the defensive reaction of the animal, to secure the survival of its species.

The heart and lungs act as logistical centres providing the necessary energy for their movements.

The logic of the animal world is bloodshed: to kill, tear apart, stifle, destroy or demolish.

The Story Of The Two Headed Creature

In the jungle, the law, of survival of the fittest reigns.

The most powerful animal and the most ferocious animal try to impose their supremacy upon the others.

The weakest animals have less of a chance to survive; they cannot escape the claws and the teeth of the predators.

The survival instinct sings behind the animal's ear; it is the first clause of the law of the jungle:

'The weak go to nothingness, the one who is not powerful will die.'

The experiences of life in the jungle teach the animals to use any available survival mechanism in the face of so many adversaries.

The more an animal's physiological capabilities are developed, the better its aggressiveness and ferociousness will express themselves.

What would happen if some day, in an extraordinary evolutionary move, the primitive brain of a reptilian predator, such as a crocodile, were set with a compact and powerful computer?

In fact, intelligence would add nothing to the physical aspect of this animal; it would only give him more possibilities to kill and demolish.

In nature, the tie between the paleocortex and the neocortex is a living example of this extraordinary connection. The new brain is a helmet made of many millions of nervous cells, with an almost endless capacity for invention and creation, and connected to the endocrine glands of the primitive brain.

From this extraordinary connection, a new creature has appeared with two heads. One of the heads was the centre of the primitive instincts and the second the centre of faculties such as the power of reasoning, imagination, calculation, the sense of association, a gigantic memory the power of analysis, speech, knowledge and hundreds of other complex capacities.

100,000 years before our era, this strange creature appeared in the jungle and, in spite of the great fragility and lightness of its bodily organs, it began with an unprecedented ferocity and nastiness to look for a place among all the other animals.

It learned its first lessons by hyenas, lions, and wolves, and organised instinctively its life according to the necessities of its merciless environment. This creature let its instinct of aggressiveness programme the cells of its neocortex according to the law of the jungle. The new brain became the servant of the hypothalamus, which began adapting its natural environment to its own taste and desires. Its daily experiences showed it that the strongest is always right. It decided to use any available means to become, apart from all creatures, the most powerful, the most cunning, and the most frightful, in order to impose its will and reign on the jungle and everywhere else.

Using its creative faculties, this double-headed creature distinguished itself from all other animals by a major difference. It reacted not only to external stimuli, but also to internal stimuli!

It felt grief, fear, violence, sadness, joy, as it hid solitary in the corner of some lost dark cave. It felt threatened by the abstract surrounding produced by its imagination, instead of fearing the concrete phenomenon of his natural environment. This creature that could hardly distinguish between the real and the imaginary and tried to make concrete its illusions in spite of external reality. It started developing its knowledge of the animal world. It began with taming the chickens, sheep, goats, horses, camels, and elephants in order to facilitate movement. It also tamed the bears, leopards, eagles, dogs and even lions to add to its destructive power in the all the confrontations it triggered against its fellow men.

Thousands of generations followed and transmitted their experiences, to allow the reptilian brain to explore and exploit the hidden corners of the neocortex better.

This double-headed creature, propelled by its carnal desires, gradually kept imposing its domination on the jungle by carving objects in stone and wood to produce arms to kill and tools for torture.

After 90,000 years, the Stone Age developed into the Age of Iron. With this fundamental evolution, the human being has served his aggressive instinct with even more sophisticated tools, made of forged iron, putting aside the previous arms and tools.

Surrounded by wild predators, the human being constantly hid his appearance behind strange masks. He was always trying to identify himself more with the other animals.

In the course of history, the human being has always been proud to share the characteristics of the wildest predators: he was happy to possess the heart of lion, the body of an elephant, the solitude of the wolf, the ferocity of the leopard.

Some thousand years more were necessary for humanity to progress once again in producing instruments of death, as it invented firearms.

In the last stage of the evolution of means of destruction, indeed, during the 20th century, humanity produced arms of mass destruction.

The human being of modern times is no less brutal than the caveman; he is simply better organised and better armed.

The human being has used time to gain control of his environment, but he has done nothing to control his reptilian brain.

Hostilities and the arms race have not given nations the time to help the evolution of their populations' consciousness. Thus, the danger of individuals in every society becoming victims of explosions of violence looms.

Those who have been condemned for committing crimes against humanity were not extra-terrestrial beings, but simple human beings who had not learned to control their carnal desires and primitive aggressive instincts.

Theses predator reptiles, hidden behind the appearance of each of these criminals, have used the daily violence of their societies. Under the leadership of these dangerous beings, individual brutal and blind violence was transformed into massive popular movements. These criminals were cunning predators capable of bewitching masses by the sole power of their words. Through hierarchical and ideological systems, they could incite and invite the masses to exercise the power of their violence in favour of the superiority of a race or a class.

The conflict between tyrants brings no legitimacy to either of them. What happened under Stalin and Hitler and under their direction is a page in the history of humanity that has not yet been turned. The same sorts of ferocity repeat themselves every day in different corners of the world: Rwanda, Cambodia, and Bosnia.

Attila, Alexander, Genghis Khan, Tamerlane, Stalin, Hitler, they all show that anyone of any nation, civilisation, or time can become an accomplished pupil at the school of savagery and murder. They only need to let themselves be directed by their primitive instincts and their reptilian brain.

One then becomes a wild beast with a human appearance very easily.

The 21st century stands before our door. The human folly has devastated the environment; the food, water and air are contaminated and carry deadly illnesses.

Modern civilisations live under the menace of blind brutality and organised violence. Poverty, individual and societal difficulties, corruption and injustice deteriorate the good relations of the citizenry.

Sanctions and hardening of the punishments are not efficient solutions to the violence that penetrates life in the cities evermore.

We are responsible for future generations.

How and with what material can we create a harmonious, healthy and long lasting society for our children?

If the educational system does not undergo a radical evolution, allowing the control of the reptilian brain, the construction of a peaceful society on the ruins of the savage world will remain an inaccessible illusion.

André Malraux, the great French philosopher, predicted that:

"The 21 century will be mystical, or it will not be."

Sufi teachings put emphasis on this prediction: by developing his soul's potentials, every human being gains consciousness of his own aptitudes beyond his ordinary faculties. He acknowledges his real spiritual dimension. He acquires self-knowledge, and how to evaluate the possibilities of his energetic body. Above all, he will recognise that he is a soul, or an energetic body, temporarily contained in a physical body for the duration of a lifetime. This certitude, born from his own direct experience, will give him not only great spiritual elation, but also a feeling of responsibility towards his fellow humans who will never go through such experiences and who go on living in the complete ignorance of things beyond.

Sufism and the Sufi method is based on and ancient maxim that says:

"Know yourself not by analogy and you will know the universe, and you will know tranquillity and peace."

Figure 11 - Shah Nematollah Wali (1329-1431).

One of the greatest Sufi Masters and the founder of Nematollahi Sufi order

www.ingramcontent.com/pod-product-compliance
Lightning Source LLC
Chambersburg PA
CBHW032114090426
42743CB00007B/345